CONTACTS

Instructor's Resource Manual

CONTACTS

Langue et culture françaises

Seventh Edition

Instructor's Resource Manual

Jean-Paul Valette
Rebecca M. Valette
Boston College

Testing Program prepared by
Andréa Javel

Video Worksheets prepared by
Nathalie Drouglazet

HOUGHTON MIFFLIN COMPANY   BOSTON   NEW YORK

Director, World Languages: New Media and Modern Language Publishing   Beth Kramer
Senior Development Editor   Cécile Strugnell
Senior Manufacturing Coordinator   Marie Barnes
Marketing Manager   José A. Mercado

Printed in the U.S.A.

ISBN: 0-618-00751-2

1 2 3 4 5 6 7 8 9-POC-05 04 03 02 01

Contents

Instructor's Guide   **IG 1**

Sample Syllabi   IG 1
Teaching a Unit   IG 8
Advice on Evaluation   IG 12
Suggestions for Realia and Secondary Sources   IG 12

Europak   **EU 1**

The Euro in Ten Questions   EU 1
La carte de l'euro   EU 6
The Euro Currency   EU 7
Euro Activities   EU 9
Euro Situations   EU 22
Euro Games   EU 28

Testing Program   **TP 1**

Introduction   TP 1

Instructor's Test Audio Script   TP 2

Test Sheets   TP 23
    Unit 1A   TP 25
    Unit 1B   TP 27
    Unit 2A   TP 29
    Unit 2B   TP 33
    Unit 3A   TP 37
    Unit 3B   TP 41
    Unit 4A   TP 45
    Unit 4B   TP 47
    Unit 5A   TP 49
    Unit 5B   TP 53
    Aperçu culturel (Version 5A)   TP 57
    Aperçu culturel (Version 5B)   TP 59
    Unit 6A   TP 61
    Unit 6B   TP 63
    Unit 7A   TP 65
    Unit 7B   TP 69
    Aperçu culturel (Version 7A)   TP 73
    Aperçu culturel (Version 7B)   TP 75
    Unit 8A   TP 77
    Unit 8B   TP 81
    Unit 9A   TP 85

Unit 9B	TP 89
Aperçu culturel (Version 9A)	TP 93
Aperçu culturel (Version 9B)	TP 95
Unit 10A	TP 97
Unit 10B	TP 101
Unit 11A	TP 105
Unit 11B	TP 109
Unit Test Answer Key	TP-AK 1

Vivre en France Oral Tests   VF 1

General Guidelines	VF 1
Unit 1	VF 3
Unit 2	VF 7
Unit 3	VF 11
Unit 4	VF 15
Unit 5	VF 19
Unit 6	VF 23
Unit 7	VF 27
Unit 8	VF 31
Unit 9	VF 35
Unit 10	VF 39
Unit 11	VF 43

Pas de problème! Video Worksheets   VW 1

To the Instructor	VW 1
Module I	VW 3
Module II	VW 5
Module III	VW 7
Module IV	VW 9
Module V	VW 11
Module VI	VW 13
Module VII	VW 15
Module VIII	VW 17
Module IX	VW 19
Module X	VW 21
Module XI	VW 23
Module XII	VW 25
Video Worksheets Answer Key	VW-AK 1

Audio Program Script   AS 1

To the Instructor	AS 1
Unité 1	AS 4
Unité 2	AS 19
Unité 3	AS 37
Unité 4	AS 57
Unité 5	AS 77
Unité 6	AS 97

Unité 7   AS 116
Unité 8   AS 139
Unité 9   AS 160
Unité 10   AS 180
Unité 11   AS 202

Song Transcript   AS 225

Lab Manual Answer Key   LM-AK 1

Pas de problème! Video Transcript   VT 1

To the Instructor   VT 1
Module I   VT 3
Module II   VT 4
Module III   VT 5
Module IV   VT 6
Module V   VT 8
Module VI   VT 10
Module VII   VT 11
Module VIII   VT 13
Module IX   VT 14
Module X   VT 15
Module XI   VT 17
Module XII   VT 18

CONTACTS

Instructor's Resource Manual

INSTRUCTOR'S GUIDE

Sample Syllabi

Preparing a Syllabus

The following sample syllabi are intended to be used as guides to accompany the seventh edition of *Contacts*. Instructors will want to adapt their syllabi to the particular needs of their program and the needs of the students to succeed in subsequent language courses. If the third and fourth semester courses stress the ability to get the gist of a text (literary or otherwise), the first-year instructor should provide the building blocks by helping students to understand and identify reading strategies that are useful when reading in a foreign language. If oral communication is the focus beyond first year, then the in-class emphasis should be on listening comprehension and oral expression. The initial dialogues or texts and the **Notes culturelles** (in French) can be used to reinforce both. Most college instructors would agree that oral expression is where most students experience difficulty and that building self-confidence in the area of speaking lowers the affective filter so that students can get the most out of their language classes.

Three-day-per-week schedule
Two semesters = 90 contact hours
Semester 1

Week	Day 1	Day 2	Day 3
1	Unit 1: Lesson 1	Lesson 1	Lesson 2
2	Lesson 2	Lesson 3	Lesson 3
3	Unit 1 Test* and **Vivre en France: Pendant le cours**	**Vivre en France:** Oral Exam	Unit 2: Lesson 4
4	Lesson 4	Lesson 5	Lesson 5
5	Lesson 6	Lesson 6	Unit 2 Test* and **Vivre en France: L'identité**
6	**Vivre en France:** Oral Exam	Unit 3: Lesson 7	Lesson 7
7	Lesson 8	Lesson 8	Lesson 9
8	Lesson 9	Unit 3 Test* and **Vivre en France: En ville**	**Vivre en France:** Oral Exam
9	Unit 4: Lesson 10	Lesson 10	Lesson 11
10	Lesson 11	Lesson 12	Lesson 12
11	Unit 4 Test	**Vivre en France: La vie à Paris**	**Vivre en France:** Oral Exam
12	Unit 5: Lesson 13	Lesson 13	Lesson 14
13	Lesson 14	Lesson 15	Lesson 15
14	Unit 5 Test	**Vivre en France: À l'hôtel**	**Vivre en France:** Oral Exam
15	Review	Review	End-of-semester Exam

*Tests for Units 1, 2, and 3 must be limited to ½ hour.

Semester 2

Week	Day 1	Day 2	Day 3
1	**Aperçu culturel: La France et ses régions**	**Aperçu culturel: La France et ses régions**	Test: **Aperçu culturel***
2	Unit 6: Lesson 16	Lesson 16	Lesson 17
3	Lesson 17	Lesson 18	Lesson 18
4	Unit 6 Test	**Vivre en France: Au café**	**Vivre en France:** Oral Exam
5	Unit 7: Lesson 19	Lesson 19	Lesson 20
6	Lesson 20	Lesson 21	Lesson 21
7	Unit 7 Test	**Vivre en France: Le courrier**	**Vivre en France:** Oral Exam
8	**Aperçu culturel: Culture et loisirs**	**Aperçu culturel: Culture et loisirs**	Test: **Aperçu culturel***
9	Unit 8: Lesson 22	Lesson 22	Lesson 23
10	Lesson 23	Lesson 24	Lesson 24
11	Unit 8 Test	**Vivre en France: Les sorties**	**Vivre en France:** Oral Exam
12	Unit 9: Lesson 25	Lesson 25	Lesson 26
13	Lesson 26	Lesson 27	Lesson 27
14	Unit 9 Test	**Vivre en France: Le sport et la santé**	**Vivre en France:** Oral Exam
15	Review	Review	End-of-semester Exam

*By omitting the tests on the **Aperçus culturels: La France et ses régions** and **Culture et loisirs,** classes meeting three days a week could complete through the **Aperçu culturel: La France, mère des arts.**

Four-day-per-week schedule
Two semesters = 120 contact hours
Semester 1

Week	Day 1	Day 2	Day 3	Day 4
1	Introduction	Unit 1: Lesson 1	Lesson 1	Lesson 2
2	Lesson 2	Lesson 3	Lesson 3	Unit 1 Test
3	**Vivre en France: Pendant le cours**	**Vivre en France:** Oral Exam	Unit 2: Lesson 4	Lesson 4
4	Lesson 5	Lesson 5	Lesson 6	Lesson 6
5	Unit 2 Test	**Vivre en France: L'identité**	**Vivre en France:** Oral Exam	Unit 3: Lesson 7
6	Lesson 7	Lesson 8	Lesson 8	Lesson 9

7	Lesson 9	Unit 3 Test	**Vivre en France: En ville**	**Vivre en France:** Oral Exam
8	Unit 4: Lesson 10	Lesson 10	Lesson 11	Lesson 11
9	Lesson 12	Lesson 12	Unit 4 Test	**Vivre en France: La vie à Paris**
10	**Vivre en France:** Oral Exam	Unit 5: Lesson 13	Lesson 13	Lesson 14
11	Lesson 14	Lesson 15	Lesson 15	Unit 5 Test
12	**Vivre en France: À l'hôtel**	**Vivre en France:** Oral Exam	**Aperçu culturel: La France et ses régions**	**Aperçu culturel: La France et ses régions**
13	Test: **Aperçu culturel**	Unit 6: Lesson 16	Lesson 16	Lesson 17
14	Lesson 17	Lesson 18	Lesson 18	Unit 6 Test
15	**Vivre en France: Au cafè**	**Vivre en France:** Oral Exam	Review	End-of-semester Exam

Semester 2

Week	Day 1	Day 2	Day 3	Day 4
1	Recap of first semester	Unit 7: Lesson 19	Lesson 19	Lesson 20
2	Lesson 20	Lesson 21	Lesson 21	Unit 7 Test
3	**Vivre en France: Le courrier**	**Vivre en France:** Oral Exam	**Aperçu culturel: Culture et loisirs**	**Aperçu culturel: Culture et loisirs**
4	**Aperçu culturel: Culture et loisirs**	Test: **Aperçu culturel**	Unit 8: Lesson 22	Lesson 22
5	Lesson 23	Lesson 23	Lesson 24	Lesson 24
6	Unit 8 Test	**Vivre en France: Les sorties**	**Vivre en France:** Oral Exam	Unit 9: Lesson 25
7	Lesson 25	Lesson 26	Lesson 26	Lesson 27
8	Lesson 27	Unit 9 Test	**Vivre en France: Le sport et la santé**	**Vivre en France:** Oral Exam
9	**Aperçu culturel: La France, mère des arts**	**Aperçu culturel: La France, mère des arts**	**Aperçu culturel: La France, mère des arts**	**Aperçu culturel: La France, mère des arts**
10	Test: **Aperçu culturel**	Unit 10: Lesson 28	Lesson 28	Lesson 29
11	Lesson 29	Lesson 30	Lesson 30	Unit 10 Test
12	**Vivre en France: En voyage**	**Vivre en France:** Oral Exam	Unit 11: Lesson 31	Lesson 31
13	Lesson 32	Lesson 32	Lesson 33	Lesson 33
14	Unit 11 Test	**Vivre en France: L'achat des vêtements**	**Vivre en France:** Oral Exam	Review
15	Review	Review	Review	End-of-semester Exam

Five-day-per-week schedule
Two semesters = 150 contact hours
Semester 1

Week	Day 1	Day 2	Day 3	Day 4	Day 5
1	Unit 1: Lesson 1	Lesson 1	Lesson 1	Lesson 2	Lesson 2
2	Lesson 2	Lesson 3	Lesson 3	Lesson 3	Unit 1 Test
3	**Vivre en France: Pendant le cours**	**Vivre en France:** Oral Exam	Unit 2: Lesson 4	Lesson 4	Lesson 4
4	Lesson 5	Lesson 5	Lesson 5	Lesson 6	Lesson 6
5	Lesson 6	Unit 2 Test	**Vivre en France: L'identité**	**Vivre en France:** Oral Exam	Unit 3: Lesson 7
6	Lesson 7	Lesson 7	Lesson 8	Lesson 8	Lesson 8
7	Lesson 9	Lesson 9	Lesson 9	Unit 3 Test	**Vivre en France: En ville**
8	**Vivre en France:** Oral Exam	Unit 4: Lesson 10	Lesson 10	Lesson 10	Lesson 11
9	Lesson 11	Lesson 11	Lesson 12	Lesson 12	Lesson 12
10	Unit 4 Test	**Vivre en France: La vie à Paris**	**Vivre en France:** Oral Exam	Unit 5: Lesson 13	Lesson 13
11	Lesson 13	Lesson 14	Lesson 14	Lesson 14	Lesson 15
12	Lesson 15	Lesson 15	Unit 5 Test	**Vivre en France: À l'hôtel**	**Vivre en France:** Oral Exam
13	**Aperçu culturel: La France et ses régions**	**Aperçu culturel: La France et ses régions**	**Aperçu culturel: La France et ses régions**	Test: **Aperçu culturel**	Unit 6: Lesson 16
14	Lesson 16	Lesson 16	Lesson 17	Lesson 17	Lesson 17
15	Lesson 18	Lesson 18	Lesson 18 (No Unit 6 test)	Review	End-of-semester Exam*

*End-of-semester Exam should include grammar, vocabulary, and culture from Unit 6.

Semester 2

Week	Day 1	Day 2	Day 3	Day 4	Day 5
1	Recap of first semester	**Vivre en France: Au café**	**Vivre en France:** Oral Exam	Unit 7: Lesson 19	Lesson 19
2	Lesson 19	Lesson 20	Lesson 20	Lesson 20	Lesson 21
3	Lesson 21	Lesson 21	Unit 7 Test	**Vivre en France: Le courrier**	**Vivre en France:** Oral Exam
4	**Aperçu culturel: Culture et loisirs**	**Aperçu culturel: Culture et loisirs**	**Aperçu culturel: Culture et loisirs**	Test: **Aperçu culturel**	Unit 8: Lesson 22
5	Lesson 22	Lesson 22	Lesson 23	Lesson 23	Lesson 23

6	Lesson 24	Lesson 24	Lesson 24	Unit 8 Test	**Vivre en France: Les sorties**
7	**Vivre en France:** Oral Exam	Unit 9: Lesson 25	Lesson 25	Lesson 25	Lesson 26
8	Lesson 26	Lesson 26	Lesson 27	Lesson 27	Lesson 27
9	Unit 9 Test	**Vivre en France: Le sport et la santé**	**Vivre en France:** Oral Exam	**Aperçu culturel: La France, mère des arts**	**Aperçu culturel: La France, mère des arts**
10	**Aperçu culturel: La France, mère des arts**	**Aperçu culturel: La France, mère des arts**	Test: **Aperçu culturel**	Unit 10: Lesson 28	Lesson 28
11	Lesson 28	Lesson 29	Lesson 29	Lesson 29	Lesson 30
12	Lesson 30	Lesson 30	Unit 10 Test	**Vivre en France: En voyage**	**Vivre en France:** Oral Exam
13	Lesson 31	Lesson 31	Lesson 31	Lesson 32	Lesson 32
14	Lesson 32	Lesson 33	Lesson 33	Lesson 33	Unit 11 Test
15	**Vivre en France: L'achat des vêtements**	**Vivre en France:** Oral Exam	Review	Review	End-of-semester Exam

Three ten-week-quarters schedule
Meet 3 times per week = 90 contact hours
Quarter 1

Week	Day 1	Day 2	Day 3
1	Unit 1: Lesson 1	Lesson 1	Lesson 2
2	Lesson 2	Lesson 3	Lesson 3
3	Unit 1 Test* and **Vivre en France: Pendant le cours**	**Vivre en France:** Oral Exam	Unit 2: Lesson 4
4	Lesson 4	Lesson 5	Lesson 5
5	Lesson 6	Lesson 6	Unit 2 Test* and **Vivre en France: L'identité**
6	**Vivre en France:** Oral Exam	Unit 3: Lesson 7	Lesson 7
7	Lesson 8	Lesson 8	Lesson 9
8	Lesson 9	Unit 3 Test* and **Vivre en France: En ville**	**Vivre en France:** Oral Exam
9	Unit 4: Lesson 10	Lesson 10	Lesson 11
10	Lesson 11	Review	End-of-quarter Exam

*Tests for Units 1, 2, and 3 must be limited to ½ hour.

Quarter 2

Week	Day 1	Day 2	Day 3
1	Lesson 12	Unit 4 Test	**Vivre en France:** **La vie à Paris**
2	**Vivre en France:** Oral Exam	Unit 5: Lesson 13	Lesson 13
3	Lesson 14	Lesson 14	Lesson 15
4	Lesson 15	Unit 5 Test	**Vivre en France:** **À l'hôtel**
5	**Vivre en France:** Oral Exam	**Aperçu culturel:** **La France et ses régions**	**Aperçu culturel:** **La France et ses régions**
6	Test: **Aperçu culturel***	Unit 6: Lesson 16	Lesson 16
7	Lesson 17	Lesson 17	Lesson 18
8	Lesson 18	Unit 6 Test	**Vivre en France:** **Au café**
9	**Vivre en France:** Oral Exam	Unit 7: Lesson 19	Lesson 19
10	Lesson 20	Review	End-of-quarter Exam

Quarter 3

Week	Day 1	Day 2	Day 3
1	Lesson 20	Lesson 21	Lesson 21
2	Unit 7 Test	**Vivre en France:** **Le courrier**	**Vivre en France:** Oral Exam
3	**Aperçu culturel:** **Culture et loisirs**	**Aperçu culturel:** **Culture et loisirs**	Test: **Aperçu culturel***
4	Unit 8: Lesson 22	Lesson 22	Lesson 23
5	Lesson 23	Lesson 24	Lesson 24
6	Unit 8 Test	**Vivre en France:** **Les sorties**	**Vivre en France:** Oral Exam
7	Unit 9: Lesson 25	Lesson 25	Lesson 26
8	Lesson 26	Lesson 27	Lesson 27
9	Unit 9 Test	**Vivre en France:** **Le sport et la santé**	**Vivre en France:** Oral Exam
10	Review	Review	End-of-quarter Exam

*By omitting the tests on the **Aperçus culturels: La France et ses régions** and **Culture et loisirs,** classes meeting three days a week could complete through the **Aperçu culturel: La France, mère des arts.**

Three ten-week-quarters schedule
Meet four times per week = 120 contact hours
Quarter 1

Week	Day 1	Day 2	Day 3	Day 4
1	Introduction	Unit 1: Lesson 1	Lesson 1	Lesson 2
2	Lesson 2	Lesson 3	Lesson 3	Unit 1 Test
3	**Vivre en France: Pendant le cours**	**Vivre en France:** Oral Exam	Unit 2: Lesson 4	Lesson 4
4	Lesson 5	Lesson 5	Lesson 6	Lesson 6
5	Unit 2 Test	**Vivre en France: L'identité**	**Vivre en France:** Oral Exam	Unit 3: Lesson 7
6	Lesson 7	Lesson 8	Lesson 8	Lesson 9
7	Lesson 9	Unit 3 Test	**Vivre en France: En ville**	**Vivre en France:** Oral Exam
8	Unit 4: Lesson 10	Lesson 10	Lesson 11	Lesson 11
9	Lesson 12	Lesson 12	Unit 4 Test	**Vivre en France: La vie à Paris**
10	**Vivre en France:** Oral Exam	Review	Review	End-of-quarter Exam

Quarter 2

Week	Day 1	Day 2	Day 3	Day 4
1	Unit 5: Lesson 13	Lesson 13	Lesson 14	Lesson 14
2	Lesson 15	Lesson 15	Unit 5 Test	**Vivre en France: À l'hôtel**
3	**Vivre en France:** Oral Exam	**Aperçu culturel: La France et ses régions**	**Aperçu culturel: La France et ses régions**	Test: **Aperçu culturel**
4	Unit 6: Lesson 16	Lesson 16	Lesson 17	Lesson 17
5	Lesson 18	Lesson 18	Unit 6 Test	**Vivre en France: Au café**
6	**Vivre en France:** Oral Exam	Unit 7: Lesson 19	Lesson 19	Lesson 20
7	Lesson 20	Lesson 21	Lesson 21	Unit 7 Test
8	**Vivre en France: Le courrier**	**Vivre en France:** Oral Exam	**Aperçu culturel: Culture et loisirs**	**Aperçu culturel: Culture et loisirs**
9	**Aperçu culturel: Culture et loisirs**	Test: **Aperçu culturel**	Unit 8: Lesson 22	Lesson 22
10	Lesson 23	Lesson 23	Review	End-of-quarter Exam

Week	Day 1	Day 2	Day 3	Day 4
1	Review: Unit 8	Lesson 24	Lesson 24	Unit 8 Test
2	**Vivre en France: Les sorties**	**Vivre en France:** Oral Exam	Unit 9: Lesson 25	Lesson 25
3	Lesson 26	Lesson 26	Lesson 27	Lesson 27
4	Unit 9 Test	**Vivre en France: Le sport et la santé**	**Vivre en France:** Oral Exam	**Aperçu culturel: La France, mère des arts**
5	**Aperçu culturel: La France, mère des arts**	**Aperçu culturel: La France, mère des arts**	**Aperçu culturel: La France, mère des arts**	Test: **Aperçu culturel**
6	Unit 10: Lesson 28	Lesson 28	Lesson 29	Lesson 29
7	Lesson 30	Lesson 30	Unit 10 Test	**Vivre en France: En voyage**
8	**Vivre en France:** Oral Exam	Unit 11: Lesson 31	Lesson 31	Lesson 32
9	Lesson 32	Lesson 33	Lesson 33	Unit 11 Test
10	**Vivre en France: L'achat des vêtements**	**Vivre en France:** Oral Exam	Oral Interviews*	End-of-quarter Exam

*Oral Interviews: Instructor could use this time to conduct oral proficiency-style interviews of his/her students, to show a French film, or to read a short literary text.

Teaching a Unit

General Ideas and Helpful (Fun) Hints

- Use realia whenever possible! These can include brochures, menus, maps, and postcards you pick up during your travels in Francophone countries, as well as ads from French magazines and newspapers.
- Put the emphasis on the visual, especially at the beginning of the semester. Use gestures, drawings, pantomime, and pictures to get your point across. When students can equate a word with something they see, the need for translation vanishes.
- Take activities out of the book and make them your own. Re-write an activity using the names of your students instead of those given. All activities are contextualized; always set the scene to introduce them as if you were telling your students a story or having a conversation with them.
- Take the dialogue that begins the lesson and make it a partial *dictée,* replacing key expressions with blanks that students fill in as they listen to the tape or CD. (A recording of each introductory dialogue is included on the Lab tape or CD for each lesson.)
- Revel in the culture! Often it is an aspect of the culture that draws students to the French language. (Teachers, too!) When covering an **Aperçu culturel,** bring in realia, food, films, and music to allow students direct contact with Francophone culture. It will motivate them to work harder on the grammar!

Sample Lesson Plan (Unit 4)

The following are suggestions for working with a typical unit in *Contacts.* The fact that certain activities are suggested, while others are omitted is a question of personal choice. These lesson plans are based on classes lasting 45–50 minutes, meeting 3 days per week. Instructors may accomplish more or less depending on time constraints and student ability.

Unit 4
Day One
Lesson 10: **Le budget de Martin**

Student Preparation for Class	In Class*
1. Read pages 134–138 in *Contacts,* noting main ideas and important grammar points (in French). 2. Analyze Martin's budget (p. 134) and **Le budget des étudiants** (p. 135) for cultural differences. 3. Write out your own monthly budget using vocabulary from page 135. 4. Do Activity 1, page 136 (to hand in).	Student budgets: Group Discussion List the items that students name on board. Comparing budgets: Pair Work** How does your budget differ from that of your partner? What expenses do you have in common? **Note culturelle:** Class Discussion Do you use an online banking system? Why or why not? Activity 1 (p. 136): Pair Work Compare your answers with your partner's and discuss the differences. Activity 3 (p. 138): Whole Group Review answers.
*All discussions should take place in French unless otherwise noted. **Instructors should circulate from group to group to make sure students are on task and to take note of common errors. Then discuss common errors and/or ideas expressed.	

Day Two
Lesson 10: **Le budget de Martin**

Student Preparation for Class	In Class
1. Workbook and Lab Manual, Lesson 10. 2. Read pages 139–145 in *Contacts,* noting main ideas and important grammar points (in French). 3. Look at Activity 9 on page 143, and decide which of the possessions mentioned you would like to have if you were a millionaire. Cut out pictures of these objects from magazines or draw them on 3 × 5 cards for use in class. 4. Translate the questions suggested in **Communications** section on page 145 into French for use in Pair Work in class.	Activity 4 (p. 139): Pair Work Set the scene by telling students how much you pay for housing each month. Ask how much they pay. Students then do Activity 4 in pairs. Activity 7 (p. 141): On a tight budget, sometimes the only solution is to borrow things from other people. In this activity see who is borrowing from whom. Activity 9 (p. 143): Role Play Pretend that you and your partner are both millionaires. Imagine that you are showing each other photos of your possessions using the pictures you prepared at home.

Instructor's Guide **IG 9**

Day Three
Lesson 11: **C'est une affaire, non?**

Student Preparation for Class	In Class
1. Read pages 146–149 in *Contacts*, noting main ideas and important grammar points (in French).	Introduction*: Instructor shows students an article of clothing, tells how much he/she paid, and asks the class *"C'est une affaire, non?"*
2. Note cultural differences found in the **Note culturelle,** page 147 (in French).	Have students read the dialogue on pages 146–147. Then ask students the questions in **Compréhension du texte** (p. 146, instructor's anno).
3. Prepare answers to the following questions: *"Avez-vous déjà fait du shopping en ligne? Qu'avez-vous acheté? À quel site Internet?"*	**Note culturelle:** Class Discussion Students discuss questions following the **Note culturelle** and their own on-line shopping habits.
4. Wear your favorite clothes to class and be prepared to describe what you're wearing.	Activity 2 (p. 149): Guided Discussion of appropriate dress for different occasions.
	Défilé de mode: In Pairs or in Front of Entire Class Model*: Instructor describes what he/she is wearing. Students take turns describing what their partner is wearing including the color, as well as other adjectives.
*Model: Instructor models use of colors and adjectives with articles of clothing.	

Day Four
Lesson 11: **C'est une affaire, non?**

Student Preparation for Class	In Class
1. Workbook and Lab Manual, Lesson 11.	Activity 4 (p. 150): Pair Work It's your birthday. Where can your friends take you? *Au théâtre? Au bowling?* In pairs, students talk about where the people in the activity are taking their friends.
2. Read pages 150–157 in *Contacts*, noting main ideas and important grammar points (in French).	
3. Prepare Activity 7, page 151, **Questions personnelles.**	Activity 7 (p. 151): In Pairs Have students compare their answers to those of their partner, and report a sample of results back to the group.
4. Translate **Communication** questions, page 157, in French in preparation for in-class activity.	**La mode** (as an alternative to activities on p. 155) Instructors model correct use of the demonstrative adjectives and the comparative, using pictures from French fashion magazines or the Internet. Model: *"Je préfère cet ensemble parce que c'est plus joli que l'autre."* Ask students which outfit (*ensemble*) they prefer and why.
	Communication (p. 157): Pair Work Before beginning the role plays, have students compare the questions they have prepared for homework with those of their neighbors.

Day Five
Lesson 12: **Le rêve et la réalité**

Student Preparation for Class	In Class
1. Read pages 158–161 in *Contacts,* noting main ideas and important grammar points (in French). 2. Prepare two difficult questions for your classmates on the **Note culturelle.** 3. Worksheet *Pas de problème!,* **Module II (Avant le visionnement).** 4. Prepare Activity 3, page 161, **Questions personnelles** and Activity 6, page 164, **Questions personnelles** to hand in.	Dialogue: Partial **Dictée** Re-type dialogue, pages 158–159, with blanks in the place of key vocabulary and grammar. Students listen to the recording. **Note culturelle:** Whole Class Divide class into two teams. Students ask each other the questions they have prepared on the **Note culturelle.** The group with the most correct answers wins a prize. **Module II,** View *Pas de problème!* Video Students use the worksheets before, during, and after viewing the video.

Day Six
Lesson 12: **Le rêve et la réalité**

Student Preparation for Class	In Class
1. Workbook and Lab Manual, Lesson 12. 2. Read pages 165–171 in *Contacts,* noting main ideas and important grammar points (in French). 3. Prepare Activity 7, page 165; Activity 9, page 166; and Activity 10, page 168.	Hand back Activities 3 and 6 (prepared for the previous class). Put common errors on overhead and discuss them briefly. Introduce the weather* with: *"Quel temps fait-il aujourd'hui?"* (p. 169). Talk about the weather and then transition to questions from Activity 13 (p. 170). Introduce **les prépositions de lieu** (p. 164). Pretend you are very disorganized and that you cannot find certain items you need to teach class. Ask students to help you find them by telling you where they are located. Model: *"Oh, là, là. Où est mon livre?"* Have one student answer. Then have students do Activity 7 (p. 165). Activity 9 (p. 166): Ask questions using *"il y a"* to see if students have the items mentioned. Activity 10 (p. 168): Groups of 3 or 4 students compare their answers to those of their classmates. Students could also take a poll regarding their preferences as a class, and put their results on the board.
*It is more natural to ask students about the weather at the beginning of a class. It transitions them from the outside world (from which they have just come), to the classroom and French.	

Day Seven
Unit 4 Test

Student Preparation for Class	In Class
Review for Unit Test.	Unit 4 Test

Day Eight
Vivre en France: La vie à Paris

Student Preparation for Class	In Class
1. Read pages 172–175 in *Contacts*.	Preparation for Oral Exam. • Assign groups for **Vivre en France** Oral Exam. • In pairs do the following activities: **Au Printemps,** page 173, and **Dans le métro,** page 175. • Bring in euros for students to look at. • Explain the exam format to students. • Run through different sections of the exam.

Day Nine
Vivre en France: Oral Exam

Student Preparation for Class	In Class
Study for Oral Exam.	**Vivre en France:** Oral Exam

Advice on Evaluation

Students may be evaluated based on the following:

Class participation and homework	20%
Workbook and Lab Manual	15%
Unit Tests	25%
Vivre en France Oral Exams	15%
Composition	5%
End-of-semester Exam	20%

Suggestions for Realia and Secondary Sources

• In Metropolitan France and **les DOM-TOM,** "Le Syndicat d'initiative" can be a good source. There is usually one in every town or region.
• The following may be purchased through **http://www.alapage.com,** the French equivalent to **http://www.amazon.com,** with great prices and low shipping costs.

CD-ROM

Musée d'Orsay: visite virtuelle/nouvelle ed., Montparnasse Multimedia, 2000
Louvre: visite virtuelle, Montparnasse Multimedia, 2000

FILM

Folly, Anne-Laure. *Femmes aux yeux ouverts,* La Médiathèque des Trois Mondes or California Newsreel*, 1993

MUSIC

l'Afro-rock: *Africa* (various artists), Putumayo World Music, 1999 (Telephone: 1-888-PUTUMAYO)
le Raï: Khaled (Cheb), *Sahra,* Universal Music, S.A., Barclay, 1996
le Rap: M.C. Solaar, *Paradisiaque,* Universal Music, S.A., Polygram, 1997
le Zouk: *Zouk* (Série Gold), Wagram Music, Last Chance Records, 1999
le Zydéco: Buckwheat, Zydeco, *Waitin' for my Ya-Ya,* Rounder Records

TRAVEL GUIDES

Gallimard publishes several series of beautiful travel guides, full of history, lovely photos, and art work. One series is called **Guides Gallimard**, and the other is called **Le Grand Guide... .** Try any or all of the following:

- *Alsace,* Collection: Guide Géographique de France, Nouveaux Loisirs, 1996
- Gleizal, Christian. *Guadeloupe: Guides Gallimard.* Paris: Gallimard, 1994
- *La Normandie,* Artoria, 1995
- *Le Grand Guide du Maroc,* Collectif, Gallimard Loisirs-Bibliothèque du voyageur, 1991
- *Le Grand Guide de Montréal,* Collectif, Gallimard Loisirs-Bibliothèque du voyageur, 1998
- *Le Grand Guide du Sénégal,* Collectif, Gallimard Loisirs-Bibliothèque du voyageur, 1999
- *Le Grand Guide du Vietnam,* Collectif, Gallimard Loisirs-Bibliothèque du voyageur, 1992
- *Martinique: Guides Gallimard,* Gallimard, 1994

OTHER BOOKS

- Droussent, C. *L'Année du cyclisme 99,* Calmann Levy, 1999
- Pivot, M. and Leven, J. *Coupe du Monde 98: Le Livre souvenir,* 1998
- Roesch, Roselyne and Rolle-Harold, Rosalba, *La France au quotidien,* Presses Universitaires de Grenoble, 2000

---

*California Newsreel is a wonderful source for African French-language films.

EUROPAK

The Euro in Ten Questions

1. What is the euro?

The **euro** is the official monetary unit of France and a number of other European countries that have adopted it as their common currency. It is divided into 100 **cents** (which are also referred to as **centimes** in France).

2. What is the symbol of the euro?

Its symbol is in the shape of the Greek letter *epsilon,* for Europa, and is crossed by two short horizontal bars.

3. Which countries use the euro?

The euro is used in twelve countries, all members of the European Union.* In addition to France, these countries are Austria, Belgium, Finland, Germany, Greece, Ireland, Italy, Luxembourg, the Netherlands (Holland), Portugal, and Spain. The euro is also used in the overseas departments of France (Martinique, Guadeloupe, Réunion, and French Guyane), as well as Saint-Pierre-et-Miquelon. The countries that use the euro constitute the Euro-Zone.

By adopting the same currency, the twelve countries of the Euro-Zone have meshed their economies very closely. These countries represent a strong economic power: they comprise approximately the same area as the eastern United States from the Atlantic to the Mississippi, but their population of about 300 million is larger than that of the entire United States.

Note: The European Union is a group of 15 European countries which have decided to partially integrate their economies, notably by eliminating most of the trade barriers among them. In addition, citizens of the European Union can study, visit, live, and work in any member country without a special visa. As of January 1, 1999, only 4 of these 15 countries had not decided to adopt the euro as their common currency: Denmark, Great Britain (England), Greece, and Sweden. Greece entered the Euro-Zone on January 1, 2001.

4. When did the euro become the official currency of France?

On January 1, 1999, the eleven charter countries of the Euro-Zone adopted the euro as their common currency. Thus, on that date, the euro became the official currency of France, replacing the franc which had been used for about 200 years. The fixed conversion rate between the two currencies was set at

1 euro = 6.55957 francs

The euro was, however, to be introduced progressively over a transition period extending from January 1, 1999, to December 31, 2001. During that period, French people would still be using francs as bank notes and coins. The new euro currency would be issued to the public only after January 1, 2002. During the transition period, however, one could write checks or make credit card purchases in either euros or francs.

January 1, 1999, through December 31, 2002	
PAYMENT BY:	CURRENCY:
• cash	*francs only*
• credit card	*euros or francs*
• check	*euros or francs*

To help French citizens become familiar with the euro and its value, prices, invoices, and bank statements would be given in both francs and the euro equivalents.

5. How and when will the transition to the euro be completed?

On January 1, 2002, the new euro bills and coins will be issued to the French public. As of July 1, 2002, the old franc currency will be completely withdrawn from circulation and the euro will be the only means of payment accepted in France. Similarly, German marks, Italian liras, Spanish pesetas, Greek drachmas, Finnish markkas, Dutch guilders, and all other currencies previously used by the Euro-Zone countries will be replaced by euros. As a result, these twelve countries will all have a single common currency.

6. What is the value of the euro?

The euro has exactly the same value in every European country where it has been adopted. That means that one euro in France has the same value as one euro in Germany, Italy, Spain, or Portugal. However, the euro does fluctuate against other world currencies. Since 1999, the value of one euro has fluctuated between approximately $1.00 and $1.90 U.S.

7. What does the euro currency consist of?

The euro currency consists of 7 different bills and 8 different coins.

    The 7 bills, which are identical in all twelve euro countries, are of different colors and different sizes, with the size increasing with the value of each bill.

Colors of Euro Currency			
5 euros	(gray)	100 euros	(green)
10 euros	(red)	200 euros	(yellow)
20 euros	(blue)	500 euros	(purple)
50 euros	(orange)		

The decision to issue bills of different sizes, which go from 5 euros (the smallest) to 500 euros (the largest), was made in order to help visually challenged people identify the denomination of each bill by feel.

    The 8 coins (1, 2, 5, 10, 20, 50 cents, and 1 and 2 euros) have the same image on the recto (or "head") side in all the countries using the euro currency. The verso (or "tail") side, however, features national symbols typical of the country in which they are minted.

8. Why did France and other European countries decide to adopt the euro?

The adoption of the euro as a common currency represents a very significant step in the economic integration of Europe. In contrast to the United States, where a single currency, the dollar, is used in every state, each of the different countries of Europe had its own national currency (such as the French franc, the German mark, and the Italian lira) which had a variable rate of exchange with all other currencies. The existence of different national currencies and the need to exchange them with one another greatly complicated the trade relationships among various countries. It also represented major costs and challenges for the millions of Europeans who work, travel, and spend vacations in countries other than their own.

European Currencies Replaced by the Euro			
Austria	the schilling	**Ireland**	the pound
Belgium	the Belgian franc	**Italy**	the lira
Finland	the markka	**Luxembourg**	the Luxembourg franc
France	the French franc	**Netherlands** (Holland)	the guilder
Germany	the mark	**Portugal**	the escudo
Greece	the drachma	**Spain**	the peseta

The adoption of a single European currency is eliminating these problems. For example, an Irish student who works during the summer in Germany as an au pair can bring back all his/her savings in euros to Ireland without having to pay a commission for changing marks into pounds. An Austrian student graduating from engineering school might find it financially rewarding to work in Finland after having searched the Internet for European job offerings and compared salaries in euros. A young French professional looking for a used Italian sports car might find it advantageous to buy it from a dealer in Portugal after having compared international listings on the Internet.

9. What are the advantages of the euro for Americans?

The main advantage of the euro is the ease and simplicity of its use. For example, American students who decide to visit Paris, Rome, Munich, and Vienna on a summer tour no longer need to change U.S. dollars into francs, francs into liras, liras into marks, and marks into schillings as they travel from city to city. They can simply buy euro traveler's checks or pay in euros with a credit card. As of January 2002, they need only carry euros in their wallets as they travel throughout the euro countries. Also, since one euro is worth approximately one dollar, it is easy to figure out how much one is spending.

10. Where can one obtain more information on the euro?

Informative sites for the euro can be found on the Internet at

http://www.laposte.fr/euro
http://www.europa.eu.int/euro

La carte de l'euro

(au 1er janvier 2001)

Les 12 pays de l'Union Européenne qui ont adopté l'euro:

- l'Autriche
- l'Allemagne
- la Belgique
- l'Espagne
- la Finlande
- la France
- la Grèce

- l'Irlande
- l'Italie
- le Luxembourg
- les Pays-Bas (la Hollande)
- le Portugal

Les 3 pays de l'Union Européenne qui n'ont pas adopté l'euro:

- le Danemark
- la Grande Bretagne

- la Suède

LA SUÈDE

LA FINLANDE

LE DANEMARK

L'IRLANDE

LA GRANDE BRETAGNE

LES PAYS-BAS

LA BELGIQUE

L'ALLEMAGNE

LE LUXEMBOURG

LA FRANCE

L'AUTRICHE

LE PORTUGAL

L'ESPAGNE

L'ITALIE

LA GRÈCE

The Euro Currency

Although the euro was adopted as the official currency of France on January 1, 1999, the new euro currency will not be issued until January 1, 2002. In the interim three-year period, the franc currency will still be in use.

The euro currency consists of 7 bills and 8 coins whose design has been approved and well-publicized in the countries of the Euro-Zone. Although each country has been authorized to print its own bills and mint its own coins, all the bills will be identical, and all the coins, although differing in their verso (or "tail") images, will be of exactly the same size and weight. The euro currency printed or minted in any one country is valid throughout the Euro-Zone.

The bills (bank notes)

The 7 bills are of different colors and different sizes, with the size increasing with the value of each bill: **5 euros** (gray), **10 euros** (red), **20 euros** (blue), **50 euros** (orange), **100 euros** (green), **200 euros** (yellow), **500 euros** (purple).

The design of the euro bills was created by an Austrian artist and is identical for all countries using the euro.

- The **doors**, **windows**, and **archways** pictured on the front (or recto) of the bills symbolize economic opportunity and the opening to new ideas.
- The **bridges** that constitute the main motif of the back (or verso) side evoke the strong ties between the European countries represented in the small map on the right of the bill.

These architectural and engineering features are not real buildings or bridges, but rather represent different styles from various periods in European history, ranging from the Roman empire (5 euros) to the present day (500 euros).

The coins

The 8 coins (**1, 2, 5, 10, 20, 50** cents, and **1** and **2 euros**) have the same image on the recto (or "head") side in all the countries using the euro currency. The verso (or "tail") side, however, features national symbols typical of the country in which they are minted. For the French coins, the verso bears the following images:

- The 1, 2, and 5 cent coins represent the face of **Marianne**,[1] symbol of the French Republic.
- The 10, 20, and 50 cent coins bear the letters **RF** (for République Française) and an effigy of **La Semeuse** (a woman sowing seeds) who has traditionally been another symbol of France.
- The 1 and 2 euro coins feature a tree of life together with the letters "RF" and the French motto **"Liberté, Égalité, Fraternité."**

---

[1] This allegorical figure first appeared on coins during the French Revolution. "Marianne" also appeared on many stamps and coins, denominated in francs.

Euro Posters

Each of the euro bank notes features a different architectural style, with drawings of doors and windows (on the front of the bill) and bridges (on the back of the bill). None of these are replicas of a specific monument in a specific country of the Euro-Zone. As a classroom project, students can create posters highlighting French monuments that illustrate the style of each bank note.

Denomination	Architectural Type	Possible Illustrations
5 euros	Gallo-Roman (1st to 4th centuries)	Arena at Nîmes; amphitheater at Orange; Pont du Gard (Roman aqueduct over the Gard)
10 euros	Romanesque (5th to 11th centuries)	Romanesque churches: e.g., in Poitiers (Notre Dame La Grande), Clermont-Ferrand (Notre Dame du Port); Pont d'Avignon (pont St. Bénézet)
20 euros	Gothic (12th to 15th centuries)	Gothic cathedrals: e.g., at Chartres, Reims, Amiens; Notre Dame de Paris; medieval bridge at Cahors
50 euros	Renaissance (16th century)	Chenonceaux, Chambord; Place des Vosges (Paris), Pont Neuf (Paris)
100 euros	Classical and Baroque (17th and 18th centuries)	Versailles; Vaux-le-Vicomte; le Louvre; Stone bridges over the Loire at Blois, Orléans
200 euros	Iron, steel, and glass (19th century)	Grand Palais; musée d'Orsay (former train station); Pont des Arts (Paris); railroad bridge by Eiffel in Auvergne near St. Flour (viaduc de Garabit)
500 euros	Highrise buildings and suspension bridges (20th and 21st centuries)	La Défense; Bibliothèque Nationale; Tour Montparnasse; Pont de Tancarville (between Le Havre and Rouen)

Counting Out Loud in Euros

In French, the word euro is pronounced /øro/. When counting, the usual rules of liaison apply. The basic liaison and linking patterns are as follows.

1 € un/n/ euro	6 € six/z/ euros	11 € onze euros	40 € quarante euros
2 € deux/z/ euros	7 € sept/t/ euros	12 € douze euros	100 € cent/t/ euros
3 € trois/z/ euros	8 € huit/t/ euros	13 € treize euros	200 € deux cents/z/ euros
4 € quatre euros	9 € neuf/v/ euros	20 € vingt/t/ euros	1000 € mille euros
5 € cinq/k/ euros	10 € dix/z/ euros	30 € trente euros	2000 € deux mille euros

Euro Activities

Writing Checks

Writing checks provides one of the most realistic contexts in which to practice written numbers. Check-writing activities can be tailored to the students' linguistic level, ranging from the simplest numbers (from 1 to 20) to the most complex (numbers above 1000).

French checks are filled out as follows.

```
┌─────────────────────────────────────────────────────────────────┐
│  CRÉDIT MUTUEL                                                     │
│  Payez contre chèque la somme de  trois cent soixante-dix euros   │
│     et vingt-cinq centimes                      ┌─────────┐        │
│                                                 │ 370,25  │ €      │
│  à l'ordre de  Claire Chauvallon                └─────────┘        │
│                      à  Grenoble                                  │
│                     le 10 mai 2001                                │
│                          Jean-Christophe Bertrand                 │
└─────────────────────────────────────────────────────────────────┘
```

ACTIVITY: MAKING A PURCHASE BY CHECK

The copymaster entitled "À vendre" invites students to select an item they wish to purchase and to write out the corresponding check in both euros and centimes. Students must be familiar with numbers from 0 to 100.

ACTIVITY: ADDITIONAL PRACTICE IN WRITING CHECKS

The second copymaster contains sample blank checks. These can be duplicated and distributed to the students. Using these checks, activities may be structured to practice specific number categories by modifying the list of items to be purchased.

PRIX	OBJETS
• de 1 à 20 euros	un CD, un livre, une collection de magazines, un tee-shirt, une cravate, un poster/une affiche
• de 20 à 50 euros	un pantalon, une chemise, une jupe, des jeans, une montre, un pull, un walkman
• de 50 à 100 euros	une raquette de tennis
• de 100 à 999 euros	une guitare, des skis, une planche à voile, un vélo, une chaîne-stéréo, une télévision, un lecteur de cassettes, un lecteur de CD
• plus de 1000 euros	un scooter, une moto, une auto, un ordinateur

Other realistic check-writing activities can be created by using realia such as

- mail-order catalogs
- department store ads
- travel brochures
- classified ads: home furnishings, automobiles, real estate, etc.

À vendre

The items below have been posted on the bulletin board of a school you are attending in Tours, France. Select an item you would like to buy and write out a check for it, using the blank check below.

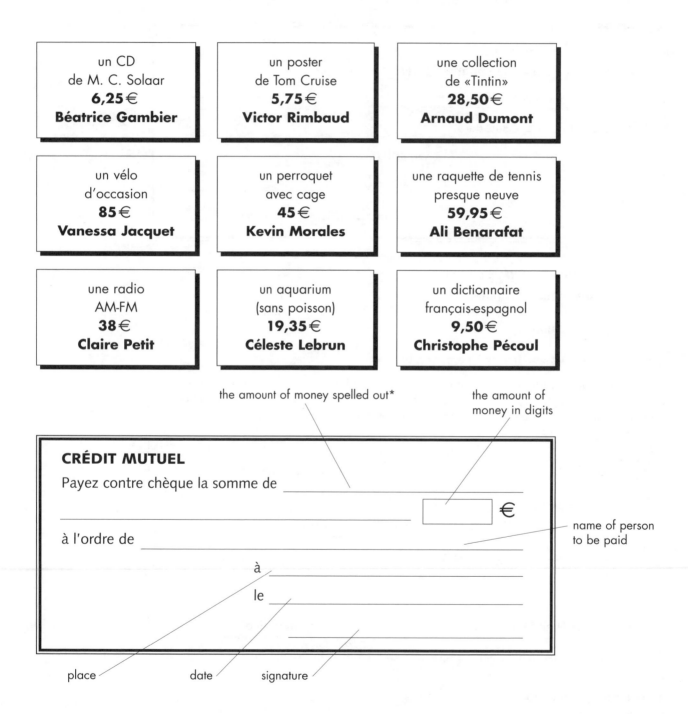

un CD
de M. C. Solaar
6,25 €
Béatrice Gambier

un poster
de Tom Cruise
5,75 €
Victor Rimbaud

une collection
de «Tintin»
28,50 €
Arnaud Dumont

un vélo
d'occasion
85 €
Vanessa Jacquet

un perroquet
avec cage
45 €
Kevin Morales

une raquette de tennis
presque neuve
59,95 €
Ali Benarafat

une radio
AM-FM
38 €
Claire Petit

un aquarium
(sans poisson)
19,35 €
Céleste Lebrun

un dictionnaire
français-espagnol
9,50 €
Christophe Pécoul

the amount of money spelled out*

the amount of money in digits

CRÉDIT MUTUEL

Payez contre chèque la somme de _____

_____ [   ] €

à l'ordre de _____

à _____

le _____

_____

name of person to be paid

place   date   signature

*Amounts in euros are written as follows:
    23,75 € = vingt-trois euros et soixante-quinze centimes

CRÉDIT MUTUEL

Payez contre chèque la somme de _____

_____ [ ] €

à l'ordre de _____

à _____

le _____

_____

✂ -

CRÉDIT MUTUEL

Payez contre chèque la somme de _____

_____ [ ] €

à l'ordre de _____

à _____

le _____

_____

✂ -

CRÉDIT MUTUEL

Payez contre chèque la somme de _____

_____ [ ] €

à l'ordre de _____

à _____

le _____

_____

✂ -

CRÉDIT MUTUEL

Payez contre chèque la somme de _____

_____ [ ] €

à l'ordre de _____

à _____

le _____

_____

Ordering Food and Beverages

Role-play activities in which students order beverages and light foods in a café can be used to practice numbers and prices. Copymasters are provided for two menus:

- **Menu A: La Terrasse Fleurie** (simple: prices given in euros only, no centimes)
- **Menu B: Le Petit Vatel** (more complex: prices given in euros and centimes)

ACTIVITY: PRACTICING NUMBERS FROM 1 TO 12

Students select one dish and one beverage from Menu A (**La Terrasse Fleurie**) and ask the server for the check.

— *Vous désirez, Monsieur/Mademoiselle?*
— *Je voudrais un sandwich au jambon et une limonade, s'il vous plaît.*
    Ça fait combien?
— *Ça fait cinq euros.*

ACTIVITY: PRACTICING NUMBERS FROM 1 TO 30

Two students each select one dish, one beverage, and one dessert from Menu A (**La Terrasse Fleurie**). One of them asks the server for the check.

— *Vous désirez, Mademoiselle?*
— *Je voudrais un hamburger, un soda et une glace à la vanille.*
— *Et vous, Monsieur?*
— *Moi, je voudrais une pizza, une limonade et une tarte maison.*
    Ça fait combien?
— *Ça fait vingt et un euros.*

ACTIVITY: PRACTICING COMPLEX NUMBERS

Students order items from Menu B (**Le Petit Vatel**) in conversations similar to those above.

Variation: the server gives change.

— *Vous désirez, Mademoiselle/Monsieur?*
— *Je voudrais une omelette au fromage, une mousse au chocolat et un café.*
— *Ça fait neuf euros et trente-cinq centimes.*
— *Voilà dix euros.*
— *Et voilà votre monnaie: soixante-cinq centimes.*
— *Merci bien.*

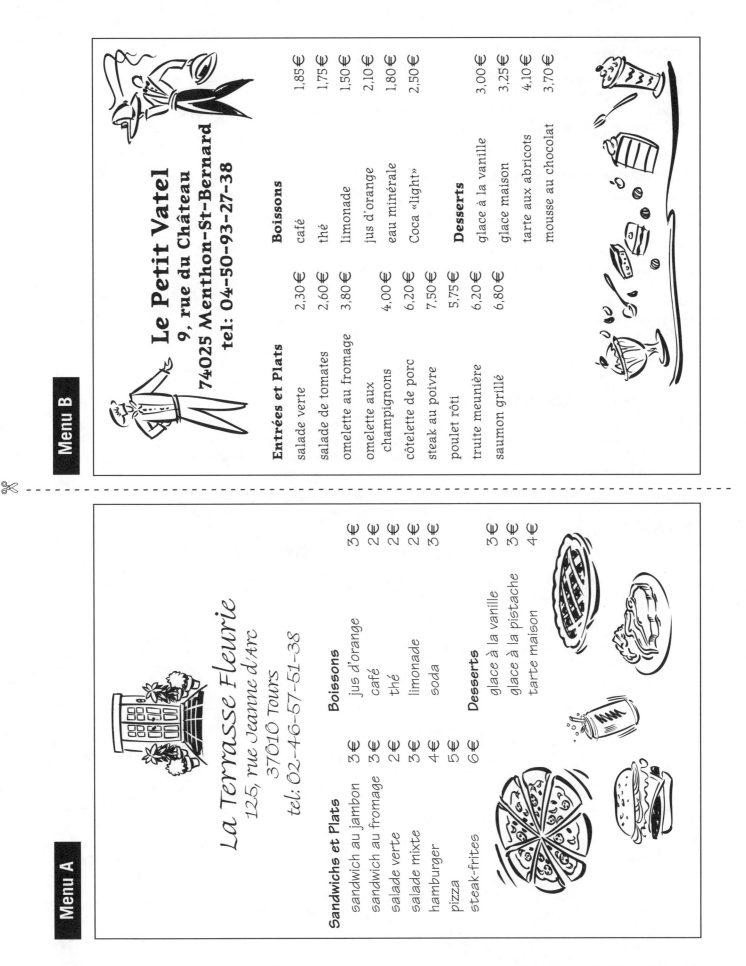

Le Petit Vatel
9, rue du Château
74025 Menthon-St-Bernard
tel: 04-50-93-27-38

Entrées et Plats

salade verte	2,30 €
salade de tomates	2,60 €
omelette au fromage	3,80 €
omelette aux champignons	4,00 €
côtelette de porc	6,20 €
steak au poivre	7,50 €
poulet rôti	5,75 €
truite meunière	6,20 €
saumon grillé	6,80 €

Boissons

café	1,85 €
thé	1,75 €
limonade	1,50 €
jus d'orange	2,10 €
eau minérale	1,80 €
Coca «light»	2,50 €

Desserts

glace à la vanille	3,00 €
glace maison	3,25 €
tarte aux abricots	4,10 €
mousse au chocolat	3,70 €

La Terrasse Fleurie
125, rue Jeanne d'Arc
37010 Tours
tel: 02-46-57-51-38

Sandwichs et Plats

sandwich au jambon	3 €
sandwich au fromage	3 €
salade verte	2 €
salade mixte	3 €
hamburger	4 €
pizza	5 €
steak-frites	6 €

Boissons

jus d'orange	3 €
café	2 €
thé	2 €
limonade	2 €
soda	3 €

Desserts

glace à la vanille	3 €
glace à la pistache	3 €
tarte maison	4 €

Shopping, Buying, and Selling

Although most students are quick to "learn" French numbers, it takes a great deal of practice for these numbers to become second nature. The activities in information gap format provide much needed practice in giving numbers out loud and in understanding numbers as they are spoken.

ACTIVITY: ASKING AND GIVING PRICES

Students each bring to class a picture of an item with a price in euros marked on the back. They ask their classmates to guess the price.

— *Combien coûte ton livre sur Paris? Trente euros?*
— *Non, c'est plus cher.*
— *Quarante euros?*
— *Non, c'est moins cher.*
— *Trente-cinq euros?*
— *Presque, mais un peu plus cher.*
— *Trente-six euros?*
— *Oui, c'est ça.*

ACTIVITY: RESPONDING TO A CLASSIFIED AD

In this activity, students in pairs take turns responding to a classified ad and asking how much the advertised items cost in euros. Prepare sufficient copies of the *petites annonces* copymaster and cut it in half so that you have versions for Students A and B. As students engage in this information gap activity, they fill in the missing information.

Variation: Students can create and distribute their own *petites annonces*. They can then engage in role-play phone conversations in which a prospective buyer calls to ask about the prices.

Petites annonces

1. You have just read the following classified ad. Call the number listed and find out the prices of the objects listed.

> Avez-vous besoin de meubles? Nous vendons, à des prix intéressants: un sofa, une table avec six chaises, deux lampes, un réfrigérateur et un lit.
> Tél: 02.35.78.02.96

sofa   _____ €
table et 6 chaises   _____ €
2 lampes   _____ €
réfrigérateur   _____ €
lit   _____ €

2. You have placed an ad in the paper to sell the following objects. You are asking the following prices. Respond to your caller's queries.

85 €

70 €

115 €

10 €

1750 €

Petites annonces

1. You have placed an ad in the paper to sell the following objects. You are asking the following prices. Respond to your caller's queries.

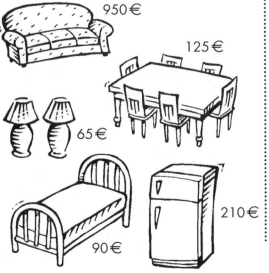

950 €

125 €

65 €

210 €

90 €

2. You have just read the following classified ad. Call the number listed and find out the prices of the objects listed.

> Aimez-vous les sports? Je vous offre un vélo presque neuf, une raquette de tennis, des skis, une très belle moto, et, pour les jeunes, un ballon de foot.
> Tél: 02.35.72.14.98

vélo   _____ €
raquette de tennis   _____ €
skis   _____ €
ballon de foot   _____ €
moto   _____ €

Finding a Place to Stay

More advanced students can engage in role-play conversations discussing euro prices in relation to hotel reservation activities.

ACTIVITY: MAKING A RESERVATION

Use the copymaster on the next page to duplicate the flyers for the two Paris hotels, and cut the sheets of paper in half. Divide the class into pairs and distribute the flyer for the **Hôtel des Artistes** to Student A and the flyer for the **Hôtel d'Italie** to Student B. In this role-play activity, Student B phones the **Hôtel des Artistes** to ask about price information and takes notes while Student A plays the part of the receptionist. Finally Student B makes a reservation for a specific type of room for specific dates. Then the roles are reversed, and Student A phones the **Hôtel d'Italie** where Student B is the receptionist. Encourage creativity in the conversations.

Variation: The type of room requested is no longer available, so the client must select another option.

ACTIVITY: SELECTING A HOTEL

In this activity, the prices and amenities of several hotels of the **Accor** chain located in the 14th and 15th **arrondissements** of Paris are to be matched with the needs of prospective clients. Prepare a sufficient number of activity sheets from the copymasters for "À la recherche d'un hôtel" so that half the class will have sheets marked "Élève A" and the other half will have sheets marked "Élève B." The instructions are on the copymasters.

ACTIVITY: RENTING AN APARTMENT

In this activity, students work in pairs reading rental ads to help one another find an apartment that fits their respective budget constraints. Prepare a sufficient number of activity sheets from the copymasters for "Appartements à louer" so that half the class will have sheets marked "Élève A" and the other half will have sheets marked "Élève B." The instructions are on the copymasters.

Variation: The budget constraints can be modified so as to change the selection of the apartment.

Hôtel des Artistes***
Tél 01 45 35 21 80

Charmant hôtel situé sur la rive gauche, quartier Saint Germain des Prés.

- Téléphone direct
- TV satellite
- Salle de bains en marbre avec sèche-cheveux
- Service bar

Tarifs

chambre simple	105 €
chambre double	120 €
chambre à deux lits	135 €
chambre double de luxe	150 €
petit déjeuner continental	8 €

(Toutes taxes comprises)

Hôtel d'Italie***
Tél 01 42 64 35 92

Élégant hôtel au cœur de Paris, près du musée d'Orsay, avec tout le confort d'hôtel de luxe:

- TV/cable, coffre-fort
- Sèche-cheveux dans chaque chambre
- Parking à proximité

Tarifs

Appartement 2 personnes	225 €
Chambre «de luxe»	145/175 €
Chambre double	100 €
Personne supplémentaire	40 €
(Possible uniquement dans les chambres à 225 et 175 €.)	
Petit déjeuner	8 €

🚫 **Les animaux ne sont pas admis.**

À la recherche d'un hôtel

You are working as a summer intern for a company in New York. Since you speak French, you have been asked to phone the French hotel group **Accor** to identify appropriate hotels for the people listed below. These are the names of the hotels that you are considering. (They are all modern hotels located in the 14th and 15th **arrondissements.**)

Sofitel Forum Rive Gauche	Mercure Montparnasse
Sofitel Porte de Sèvres	Mercure Tour Eiffel
Novotel Porte d'Orléans	Mercure Paris XV
Novotel Vaugirard	Ibis Brancion

Call your partner (who is working for **Accor**), determine which hotel you think would be best for each person, and make a reservation. Next to each name, write down the name of the hotel, the date(s), and the price per night.

Barbara Corvallis will be traveling in July. She is looking for a not too expensive room, but she definitely wants air conditioning. If possible, she would prefer a hotel with a restaurant.

HÔTEL: _____

PRIX: _____

DATE(S): _____

KEY

🍽️ restaurant

🚴 salle de remise en forme

🏊 piscine

🅿️ parking

❄️ climatisation

David Levine has had health problems and his doctor has him on a daily exercise regime. He is looking for a hotel with a fitness room ("Salle de remise en forme") and a swimming pool.

HÔTEL: _____

PRIX: _____

DATE(S): _____

Maria Hurtado is passing through Paris on an extended business trip. She has a car. She would like a hotel with exercise facilities and a restaurant. However, she is on a budget and so would like to find the least expensive hotel with the above options.

HÔTEL: _____

PRIX: _____

DATE(S): _____

Kevin Leary will be spending a weekend in Paris in November. Since this portion of the trip is not covered by his expense account, he would like you to find him an inexpensive hotel. He will get his exercise by visiting Paris on foot, and is eager to explore the lesser-known restaurants that the city has to offer.

HÔTEL: _____

PRIX: _____

DATE(S): _____

À la recherche d'un hôtel

Élève B

You are working for the **Accor** hotel company in Paris. Respond to the questions of the young intern who is calling you from New York by referring to the chart below.

	🍽	🚴	🏊	🅿	❄	PRIX
1 Sofitel Forum Rive Gauche	x	x		x	x	200–230 €
2 Sofitel Porte de Sèvres	x	x	x	x	x	240–330 €
3 Novotel Porte d'Orléans	x			x	x	115–180 €
4 Novotel Vaugirard	x	x		x	x	155–170 €
5 Mercure Montparnasse	x			x	x	175 €
6 Mercure Tour Eiffel				x		150 €
7 Mercure Paris XV				x		105–110 €
8 Ibis Brancion						65–70 €

Réservations:

Nom du client	Date(s)	Nom de l'hôtel	Prix

KEY	🍽 restaurant	🚴 salle de remise en forme	🏊 piscine	🅿 parking	❄ climatisation

Appartements à louer

(1)

You and your partner are helping each other find an apartment in Paris by reading the classified ads from two different newspapers. You can only pay around 580 euros a month rent. Ask your partner about the prices of the four apartments (A, B, C, and D) that he/she found in the paper.

Appartement A: _____ €   Appartement C: _____ €

Appartement B: _____ €   Appartement D: _____ €

After you have found the apartment with the rent you want to pay, ask three questions to find out more about the apartment, and note the information below.

Appartement _____

_____

_____

_____

(2)

Now your partner will ask you information about the following ads that you have found.

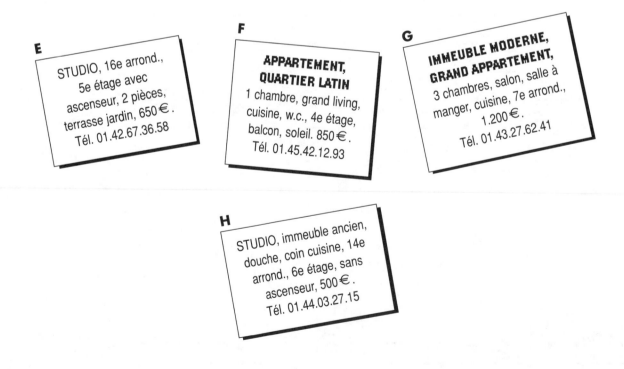

E
STUDIO, 16e arrond., 5e étage avec ascenseur, 2 pièces, terrasse jardin, 650 €. Tél. 01.42.67.36.58

F
APPARTEMENT, QUARTIER LATIN
1 chambre, grand living, cuisine, w.c., 4e étage, balcon, soleil. 850 €. Tél. 01.45.42.12.93

G
IMMEUBLE MODERNE, GRAND APPARTEMENT,
3 chambres, salon, salle à manger, cuisine, 7e arrond., 1.200 €. Tél. 01.43.27.62.41

H
STUDIO, immeuble ancien, douche, coin cuisine, 14e arrond., 6e étage, sans ascenseur, 500 €. Tél. 01.44.03.27.15

Appartements à louer

(1)

You and your partner are helping each other find an apartment in Paris by reading the classified ads from two different newspapers. Your partner will ask you information about the following ads that you have found.

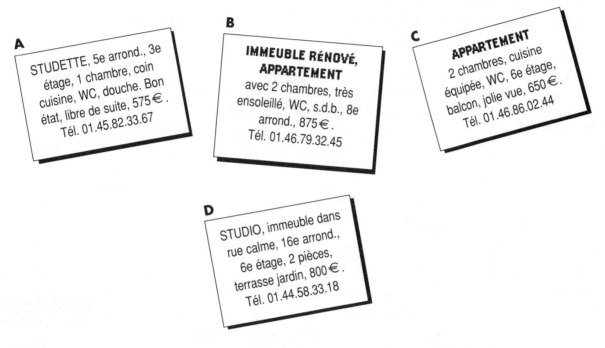

A STUDETTE, 5e arrond., 3e étage, 1 chambre, coin cuisine, WC, douche. Bon état, libre de suite, 575 €. Tél. 01.45.82.33.67

B IMMEUBLE RÉNOVÉ, APPARTEMENT avec 2 chambres, très ensoleillé, WC, s.d.b., 8e arrond., 875 €. Tél. 01.46.79.32.45

C APPARTEMENT 2 chambres, cuisine équipée, WC, 6e étage, balcon, jolie vue, 650 €. Tél. 01.46.86.02.44

D STUDIO, immeuble dans rue calme, 16e arrond., 6e étage, 2 pièces, terrasse jardin, 800 €. Tél. 01.44.58.33.18

(2)

Now you are trying to find a comfortable apartment costing about 800 euros a month. Ask your partner about the prices of the four apartments (E, F, G, and H) that he/she found in the paper.

Appartement E: _____ €

Appartement G: _____ €

Appartement F: _____ €

Appartement H: _____ €

After you have found the apartment with the rent you want to pay, ask three questions to find out more about the apartment, and note the information below.

Appartement _____

_____

_____

_____

Euro Situations

These conversation-card activities are designed for pair work. The instructions are in English, thus encouraging students to select appropriate vocabulary and structures so as to express themselves in a comprehensible manner.

IMPORTANT NOTE: If students do not know a specific word or expression, encourage them to paraphrase using familiar vocabulary.

The cards are grouped in three levels. The conversational situations in Niveau 1 use only the present tense and the future with *aller*. Those in Niveau 2 use the past tense: imperfect or passé composé. The situations in Niveau 3 require a somewhat broader vocabulary.

DIRECTIONS TO THE STUDENT: Read the instructions on the cards below and ask your partner the questions in French. Your partner will play the role of the other person in the situation and answer the questions. Take turns asking and answering the questions. Make sure to use euros when answering questions about money.

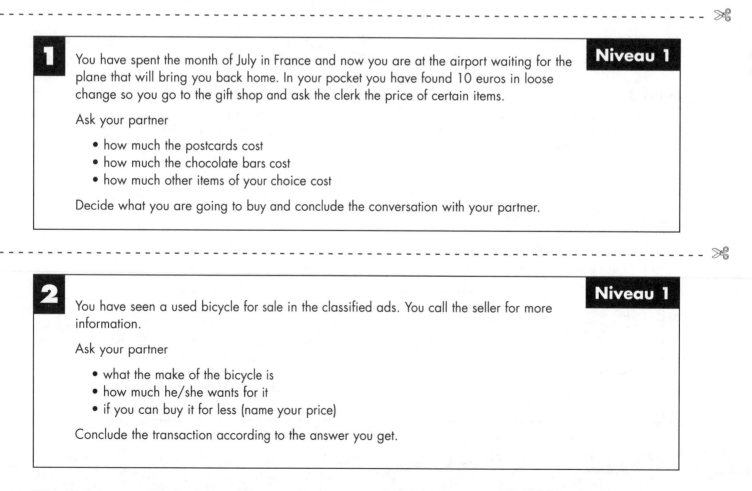

1   **Niveau 1**

You have spent the month of July in France and now you are at the airport waiting for the plane that will bring you back home. In your pocket you have found 10 euros in loose change so you go to the gift shop and ask the clerk the price of certain items.

Ask your partner

- how much the postcards cost
- how much the chocolate bars cost
- how much other items of your choice cost

Decide what you are going to buy and conclude the conversation with your partner.

2   **Niveau 1**

You have seen a used bicycle for sale in the classified ads. You call the seller for more information.

Ask your partner

- what the make of the bicycle is
- how much he/she wants for it
- if you can buy it for less (name your price)

Conclude the transaction according to the answer you get.

3 You have a very good friend who often borrows money and sometimes returns it late. Once again he/she is approaching you for a loan.

Ask your partner

- how much money he/she needs
- what for
- when he/she is going to give you back the money

Decide what to do on the basis of your partner's answers and conclude the conversation accordingly.

---

4 A good friend calls you to go to the movies tonight. You would like to go but cannot find your wallet.

Ask your partner

- what movie he/she wants to see
- how much the tickets cost
- if he/she can lend you the money

According to your partner's response, either set up a time and place where you will meet, or politely decline the invitation.

---

5 Your favorite aunt is going to celebrate her 40th birthday in a few weeks and you would like to give her a nice present. You want to spend about 40 euros. You go to a shop and talk to the salesperson.

Ask your partner

- how much the perfume "Nirvana" costs (it's your aunt's favorite!)
- how much a scarf by "Janelle" costs
- how much another present of your choice costs

Make a purchase decision and conclude the conversation.

---

6 You have heard that your favorite rock band, the "Zazoos," will be in town soon. You call the box office to know more about their performance.

Ask your partner

- when the Zazoos are going to give their concert
- how much the tickets cost
- if there is a special price for students and how much it is

Conclude your conversation by reserving the number of tickets you need.

Europak: Euro Situations **EU 23**

1   **Niveau 2**

At the flea market, you stop by a stand that is selling posters of old movie stars. You are particularly interested in a poster that would look great in your room and want to get it for a price you can afford.

Ask your partner

- who the movie star is in the poster
- what movies he/she played in
- what the price of the poster is

Ask for a better price and continue the conversation until you come to an acceptable arrangement.

---✂

2   **Niveau 2**

After soccer practice, your friend discovers that his/her wallet is missing.

Ask your partner

- how much money he/she had in the wallet
- if he/she needs money
- how much he/she needs to go home by bus

According to your friend's answers, lend him/her the money requested.

---✂

3   **Niveau 2**

Your French friend is selling his/her in-line skates (**les rollers**).

Ask your friend

- when he/she bought the skates
- how much he/she paid for them
- how much he/she wants for them

Offer a lower price and continue the conversation until you agree on an acceptable price.

---✂

4   **Niveau 2**

Every year you solicit door to door for the French Red Cross (**la Croix rouge**). You knock at the door of a wealthy and generous contributor.

Ask your partner

- how much money he/she gave last year
- how much he/she is going to give this year
- if he/she can give more, adding a reason why the gift is needed

Conclude the conversation by thanking your generous contributor.

5

For your birthday you received 70 euros with which you want to buy a portable CD player (**un discman**). You go to a discount electronics store and talk to a salesperson.

Ask your partner

- what the least expensive brand is
- how much it costs
- what the next model up is and how much it costs

Make a decision about what to buy and make your purchase.

6

You accidently broke the camera that you borrowed from a friend. You apologize and want to pay him/her back for the loss of the camera.

Ask your partner

- where and when he/she bought the camera
- how much he/she paid for it
- what the price of a new camera is

Continue the conversation until you come to a fair settlement.

7

You are in Paris with a friend who knows the city very well. You want to enjoy your visit but you do not want to spend too much money.

Ask your partner

- how much it costs to go up the Eiffel Tower
- how much it costs to go for a ride in a **bateau-mouche**
- the price of another activity you are interested in doing

Depending on what you like to do and how much you are willing to spend, make your plans for the day.

8

You and your friends had a light lunch at a café. To pay the total bill, they all chipped in, but not necessarily according to the price of what they had ordered. You are handling the money and are trying to straighten things out.

Ask your partner

- what he/she ordered
- how much it cost
- how much he/she paid

Depending on whether your partner overpaid or underpaid his/her share of the bill, you will ask for more money or return the amount due.

Europak: Euro Situations **EU** 25

1 **Niveau 3**

You own a villa in southern France and have hired a French teenager to take care of your garden. It is the end of the first week and you are talking with him/her as to how much is owed for the work done.

Ask your partner

- what he/she did in the garden
- how many hours he/she worked this week
- how much he/she charges per hour

Conclude the conversation by paying your partner the amount requested, or by arguing with him/her if you feel you have been overcharged.

---

2 **Niveau 3**

In a store that often offers sales, you have seen a jacket you like very much. You talk to the salesperson about the price.

Ask your partner

- what the price of the jacket is
- when the store is going to have its next sale
- how much the jacket will cost on sale

Decide what to do and conclude the conversation accordingly.

---

3 **Niveau 3**

Next week you will be visiting Annecy and you phone the **Hôtel Mercure** to make a reservation.

Ask your partner

- if they have rooms available next Monday
- how much the rooms cost
- how much breakfast costs
- if there is a reduction if you stay two or more days, and if so how much it is

Decide how many days you will stay and make your reservation.

---

4 **Niveau 3**

The computer you bought two years ago needs to be repaired. You bring it to a shop that fixes old computers and sells new ones.

Ask your partner

- when they can repair your computer
- how much the repair is going to cost
- what the price of a new computer is

Come to a decision on the basis of your partner's answers and conclude the conversation accordingly.

---

5   You left your old moped at the local repair shop for its annual check-up. Today you pick up the moped and talk to the assistant manager of the shop.

Ask your partner

- what they fixed
- how long they worked on the moped
- how much you owe them

Complain that the repair is too expensive and continue the conversation until you come to an agreement.

---

6   An ad agency is recruiting students to work in their mailroom this summer. You are interested in the job and phone for more information.

Ask your partner

- how many weeks they need students
- how much they pay per hour
- when you can come for an interview

Set up a date and time, and conclude the conversation politely.

---

7   You are a middle-management executive in a French company and have decided to hire a personal assistant to help you get things done. You are interviewing a prospective candidate.

Ask your partner

- his/her name, age, and where he/she is from
- if and where he/she has worked before
- what he/she knows how to do
- how much he/she wants to earn

Conclude the dialogue by hiring or dismissing the candidate according to his/her answers.

---

8   On weekends, your friend works as an assistant salesperson in a department store.

Ask your partner

- how many hours he/she worked last weekend
- how much money he/she earned
- what he/she plans to do with the money

Conclude the conversation by commenting on how you would spend an equivalent sum of money.

    Europak: Euro Situations   **EU**   **27**

Euro Games

Le jeu de la Bourse

This game can be used to introduce more advanced students to the French economy. Students "invest" 100,000 euros in a "portfolio" of French stocks and follow its evolution over a four-week period.

HOW TO PLAY

The teacher gives each student a copy of the "jeu de la Bourse" worksheet (on copymaster) and then divides the class into "investment teams" of 2 or 3 students each. On an overhead transparency the teacher displays the current stock market values (in euros) of the 10 French companies quoted daily in the *New York Times*. The students enter the date and the current stock prices on their worksheets. Then each team decides which stocks to buy so that their total investment is close to (but not above) 100,000 euros. At the end of four weeks, the teams "sell off" their portfolios at the current stock values and calculate how much money they have earned or lost. The team with the best showing is the winner.

Variation: Once a week, students are given the opportunity to modify their portfolios, buying and selling stocks at their new current value. (For this, students will need to use more complex worksheets.)

Expanded research:

a) The teacher tracks the French stocks for several weeks prior to beginning the class activity. The initial transparency could then have a series of prices for each stock, so that the teams can study the trends before making their initial investment.

b) In anticipation of the game, the teacher assigns the ten French companies to ten students (or teams of students) so that they can prepare short presentations on each company: its background, its products, and its recent performance in the stock market.

Le jeu de la Bourse

How would you do investing in the French stock market? (The performances of the following ten French companies are quoted daily in the *New York Times* and the *Wall Street Journal.*)

Air Liquide	chemicals
Alcatel Alsthom	manufacturing
AXA	life insurance
Carrefour	supermarket chain
Elf Aquitaine	petroleum
L'Oréal	beauty products
LVMH Moet He [Louis Vuitton Moët Hennessey]	luxury products
Saint Gobain	glass, chemicals
Total Fr Petr B [Total France Pétrole B]	petroleum
Gen des Eaux [La Générale des Eaux]	water utilities

Imagine you have 100,000 euros to invest. Decide which of the stocks you will buy and in what quantity. Then wait a month and see how well you have done. Who in the class has made the best investments?

DATE #1: _____

STOCK	PRICE	QUANTITY BOUGHT	TOTAL PURCHASE PRICE
Air Liquide			
Alcatel Alsthom			
AXA			
Carrefour			
Elf Aquitaine			
L'Oréal			
LVMH Moet He			
Saint Gobain			
Total Fr Petr B			
Gen des Eaux			
TOTAL INVESTMENT			_____
+ Left-over euros			+ _____
INITIAL INVESTMENT			100,000 euros

NOM _____ CLASSE _____ DATE _____

Le jeu de la Bourse *(continued)*

DATE #2: _____ (ONE MONTH LATER)

STOCK	PRICE	QUANTITY OWNED	TOTAL SALE PRICE
Air Liquide			
Alcatel Alsthom			
AXA			
Carrefour			
Elf Aquitaine			
L'Oréal			
LVMH Moet He			
Saint Gobain			
Total Fr Petr B			
Gen des Eaux			
TOTAL AMOUNT REALIZED			_____
+ Left-over euros			+ _____
TOTAL AMOUNT ON HAND			

Amount of money earned/lost _____

Who were the wisest investors in the class? _____

_____

TESTING PROGRAM

Introduction

Unit Tests: The new Testing Program for the seventh edition of *Contacts,* includes twenty-two unit tests, two versions (versions A and B) for each of the 11 units in the text. There is no difference in difficulty between versions A and B. The two versions simply allow instructors to give different tests in classes with multi-section courses. Instructors may also pick and choose items from these alternate tests to create a single test to mirror what they have covered in the classroom. Each of the unit tests contains listening comprehension activities, questions about culture (drawn either from the **Aperçus culturels** in Units 1, 2, and 3 or the **Notes culturelles** in subsequent units), and items that test understanding and knowledge of the vocabulary and grammar from that unit. The emphasis throughout is on reinforcing nascent listening comprehension and writing skills, with a gradually increasing emphasis on creating and making meaning with the language.

Administering the Unit Tests: The listening comprehension sections of the unit tests are available on cassette. Each section is read twice in succession by native speakers. The audio script for these tests is also included in the Instructor's Resource Manual, in the event the instructor prefers to read the texts aloud to his or her students. The earlier unit tests may be completed within 35 to 40 minutes, with time left to practice the survival skills presented in **Vivre en France** in preparation for the oral tests. Later tests will require approximately 40 minutes.

Vivre en France Exams: There are also 11 oral exams for the **Vivre en France** sections at the end of each unit. These exams are interactive and based on the survival skills which are the focus of **Vivre en France**. Due to the nature of these exams, additional suggestions for setting up and carrying out these exams are provided.

Aperçus culturels: There are 6 tests, i.e., two versions for each section for the **Aperçus culturels** following Units 5, 7, and 9. The **Aperçus culturels** tests have no listening component. As a change of pace, instructors may decide not to administer formal tests on these sections, preferring a less-structured format where students can experience the culture firsthand (i.e., tasting food from the different regions, seeing footage from the *Coupe du monde,* or taking a virtual visit to the Louvre or the Musée d'Orsay).

Answer Key: An answer key is included for both the unit tests and the **Aperçus culturels** tests to facilitate the task of correction for the instructor. In many cases sample answers are provided for sections that are more open-ended, but are offered merely as a guide. Instructors may choose to require more involved responses from their students based on the level of a given class.

Grading: All of the tests in the Test Bank for the seventh edition of *Contacts* are based on 100 points to facilitate grading. Sections are weighted according to difficulty, although instructors may wish to ascribe more weight to certain sections and less to others based upon the focus of their courses.

Instructor's Test Audio Script

Instructions: Listen carefully to each question. Individual items of the questions will be read twice in succession. There will be a pause to allow you to answer on your answer sheet. When the test is finished, all questions will be read through once more so that you can check your answers.

Unit Test 1A

A. Qui est-ce? You work at the reception desk of the Hôtel Ritz. You are on the phone and must complete the list of celebrity guests you hear. Each last name will be spelled out for you twice.

1. Luc Besson
2. Patrick Modiano
3. Sandrine Bonnaire

4. Gérard Depardieu
5. Virginie Ledoyen
6. Juliette Binoche

B. Une lettre. You will hear a letter Moustafa is writing to his American penpal. As you see, the letter is incomplete. Fill in the missing words and/or phrases by listening to the tape.

Cher John,

Salut! Comment ça va? Je vais comme ci comme ça. J'habite à Paris, mais je ne suis pas français. Je suis algérien. J'aime bien la musique américaine, mais je préfère le raï parce que c'est une musique algérienne. Je n'aime pas tellement les films romantiques. Je déteste le Front national. Et toi?

À bientôt!

Amitiés,
Moustafa

C. Bonjour! You're going to hear part of a conversation. Write what you hear on the line marked "A" and then complete the conversation with expressions from Unit 1 on line "B."

1. A) Bonjour, Sophie. Ça va?
2. A) Édouard, je te présente ma copine, Élisabeth.
3. A) Comment vous appelez-vous?
4. A) Merci, Christine.

Unit Test 1B

A. Qui est-ce? You work at the reception desk of the Hôtel Ritz. You are on the phone and must complete the list of celebrity guests you hear. Each last name will be spelled out for you.

1. Pascale Bussières
2. Élodie Bouchez
3. Daniel Auteuil

4. Isabelle Huppert
5. Jean Reno
6. Francis Veber

B. Une lettre. You will hear a letter Simone is writing to her American penpal. As you see, the letter is incomplete. Fill in the missing words and/or phrases by listening to the tape.

Chère Britney,

Salut! Comment vas-tu? Je vais bien. J'habite à Fort-de-France; c'est à la Martinique. Je suis martiniquaise. J'adore la musique américaine et la musique française. J'aime bien les concerts et le cinéma. Je préfère le cinéma français. Je n'aime pas tellement le sport. Je déteste la violence et le racisme. Et toi?

À bientôt.

Bien amicalement,
Simone

C. Bonjour! You're going to hear part of a conversation. Write what you hear on the line marked "A" and then complete the conversation with expressions from Unit 1 on line "B."

1. A) Bonjour, je m'appelle Sophie. Et toi?
2. A) Oui, ça va bien. Et toi?
3. A) Bonjour. Je vous présente mon ami, Pierre.
4. A) Au revoir, Jean-Paul.

Unit Test 2A

A. Visitons les pays francophones! In Unit 2 we have investigated the Francophone world. You will hear five short descriptions. Listen carefully to the descriptions and then choose the most logical answer.

MODEL:

0. Je parle français et créole. Je suis d'origine africaine.   You would mark (d) for **en Haïti.**

1. Je parle français, j'habite en Afrique et j'étudie à l'Université de Dakar.
2. J'habite en France, mais j'adore la culture américaine. Je veux travailler dans une école ou dans une compagnie internationale.
3. Je parle allemand, français et anglais. Je n'habite pas en France.
4. Je parle français et j'habite en Afrique du Nord. J'aime écouter le raï.
5. J'aime bien la musique et la cuisine cajun. Je parle français, mais je suis américaine.

B. Quelle heure est-il? Below are six clock faces, each identified by a letter. As you hear each time stated, select the corresponding clock and write the letter on your answer sheet. First, listen to the model.

MODEL:

0. Il est trois heures.   You would write **B** because picture "B" shows 3 o'clock. Then write in the other letters as you listen to the speaker.

1. Il est dix heures.
2. Il est une heure et demie.
3. Il est quatre heures et quart.
4. Il est huit heures vingt.
5. Il est minuit.

C. Trois amies. You will hear six statements about the activities of three apartment mates. If all of them are performing the activity, mark the first row: **pluriel.** If only one person is performing the activity, mark the second row: **singulier.** If it is impossible to tell, mark the third row: **impossible à dire.**

MODELS:

0. Elles habitent à Nice.   You would mark **pluriel.**
00. Elle(s) ne parle(nt) pas français.   You would mark **impossible à dire.**

1. Normalement, elles aiment regarder la télévision le soir.
2. Le matin, elles écoutent la radio.
3. Elle(s) joue(nt) au tennis le samedi.
4. Elle étudie beaucoup le week-end.
5. Le samedi après-midi, elles invitent des amis.
6. Le dimanche, elle aime parler au téléphone.

D. Mathieu. You will hear five sentences about Mathieu, each one containing a number. Listen carefully and write the appropriate numeral in the corresponding blank.

MODEL:

0. Il rentre à 18 heures.   You would mark **18** in the blank.

1. Il ne dîne pas avant <u>20</u> heures.
2. Il regarde *Friends* à la télé à <u>19</u> heures.
3. Il habite <u>192</u>, boulevard Saint Michel.
4. Il habite l'appartement numéro <u>13</u>.
5. Il travaille <u>35</u> heures par semaine.

E. La réponse est non! Let's disagree! Listen carefully to each sentence and then write the opposite (the negative form). *Do not* write the affirmative form.

MODEL:

0. J'étudie.   You write: **Je n'étudie pas.**

1. J'aime écouter le rap.
2. Ils sont au Canada.
3. Vous voyagez beaucoup.

4. Tu parles bien français.
5. Nous arrivons à 22h.

F. Questions personnelles. Your professor finds you fascinating. Answer the following questions in complete sentences so he or she can get to know you.

1. Quel jour sommes nous aujourd'hui?
2. À quelle heure est-ce que vous arrivez à l'université?
3. Qu'est-ce que vous regardez à la télé le lundi?
4. Avec qui est-ce que vous habitez?
5. Est-ce que vous aimez voyager?
6. Quand est-ce que vous étudiez?

Unit Test 2B

A. Visitons les pays francophones! In Unit 2 we have investigated the Francophone world. You will hear five short descriptions. Listen carefully to the descriptions and then choose the most logical answer.

MODEL:

0. Je parle français et créole. Je suis d'origine africaine. Kerlyne habite probablement _____.

   You would mark (d) for **en Haïti.**

1. Je suis bilingue. Je parle français et anglais, mais je préfère parler français. J'aime beaucoup ma culture.
2. Je veux être docteur. J'adore la biologie. Je veux travailler dans un hôpital.
3. Je parle allemand, mais on parle très bien français où j'habite. J'étudie l'anglais parce que je veux travailler dans une compagnie internationale.
4. Je suis bilingue. Je parle français et arabe.
5. J'adore les ordinateurs. Je veux travailler chez Microsoft.

B. Quelle heure est-il? Below are six clock faces, each identified by a letter. As you hear each time stated, select the corresponding clock and write the letter on your answer sheet. First, listen to the model.

MODEL:

0. Il est dix heures.   You would write **F** because picture "F" shows 10 o'clock. Then write in the letters
                             as you listen to the speaker.

1. Il est neuf heures.
2. Il est onze heures moins le quart.
3. Il est trois heures et demie.

4. Il est midi.
5. Il est deux heures vingt-cinq.

C. Trois amis. You will hear six statements about the activities of three apartment mates. If all of them are performing the activity, mark the first row: **pluriel.** If only one person is performing the activity, mark the second row: **singulier.** If it is impossible to tell, mark the third row: **impossible à dire.**

MODELS:

 0. Ils habitent à Paris.   You would mark **pluriel.**
00. Il(s) ne parle(nt) pas anglais.   You would mark **impossible à dire.**

1. Normalement, il(s) rentre(nt) à la maison à 18 heures.
2. Le jeudi, ils arrivent à 18 heures 30.

3. Il aime dîner à 20 heures.
4. Le soir, ils écoutent la radio.
5. Le vendredi, il invite des amis.
6. Le samedi après-midi, il(s) joue(nt) au Frisbee.

D. La vie de Christine. You will hear five sentences about Christine's life, each one containing a number. Listen carefully and write the appropriate numeral in the corresponding blank.

MODEL:

0. Elle travaille à quatre heures.   You would write **4** in the blank.

1. Christine dîne à 19 heures.   4. Elle habite l'appartement numéro 72.
2. Elle ne regarde pas la télé après 23 heures.   5. Elle travaille 47 heures par semaine.
3. Elle habite 95, avenue du Maine.

E. La réponse est non! Let's disagree! Listen carefully to each sentence and then write the opposite (the negative form). *Do not* write the affirmative form.

MODEL:

0. J'étudie.   You write: **Je n'étudie pas.**

1. Vous chantez bien.   4. Roméo aime regarder Juliette.
2. Je suis à Montréal.   5. Tu regardes souvent la télé.
3. Pierre invite Paul.

F. Questions personnelles. Your professor finds you fascinating. Answer the following questions in complete sentences so he or she can get to know you.

1. Quelle est la date aujourd'hui?   4. Où est-ce que vous habitez?
2. Quel jour de la semaine sommes-nous?   5. Est-ce que vous aimez danser?
3. Comment vous appelez-vous?   6. Est-ce que vous êtes américain(e)?

Unit Test 3A

A. Des amis. You will hear five statements about various people. If the noun in the sentence is masculine, mark row one: **masculin.** If the noun in the sentence is feminine, mark row two: **féminin.** If it is impossible to tell, mark the third row: **impossible à dire.**

MODELS:

 0. Dominique est français.   You would mark row one for **masculin.**
00. C'est une bonne copine.   You would mark row two for **féminin.**

1. Daniel(èle) est poli(e).   4. Ce sont des ami(e) espagnol(e)s.
2. C'est une petite télévision.   5. Ce sont des étudiants dynamiques.
3. Voici un copain japonais.

B. Logique ou illogique? You will hear five pairs of sentences. For each pair, decide whether the second action logically follows the first action, and mark either **logique** or **illogique** on the chart below.

MODEL:

0. Anne va au restaurant. Elle va dîner avec un copain.   You would mark row one for **logique.**

1. Je vais à Nice en train. Je vais à la gare.
2. Marie va jouer au football. Elle va à l'aéroport.
3. Nous allons au bureau dimanche. Nous ne travaillons pas beaucoup.
4. Gérard va à la plage. Il va nager.
5. Ils aiment aller au cinéma. Ils vont rester à la maison.

C. Une chambre d'étudiant(e). Answer the following questions affirmatively or negatively according to the picture below.

MODEL:

0. Est-ce qu'il y a des livres?   You would mark: **Oui, il y a des livres.**

1. Est-ce qu'il y a une guitare?
2. Est-ce qu'il y a un lecteur de CD-ROM?
3. Est-ce qu'il y a une moto?

4. Est-ce qu'il y a un téléphone?
5. Est-ce qu'il y a un caméscope?

D. Demain aussi. Listen to what the following people are doing. Then say that tomorrow they are going to do the same things.

MODEL:

0. Je joue du piano.   You would write: **Demain aussi, je vais jouer du piano.**

1. Nathalie utilise son ordinateur.
2. Nous jouons aux échecs.
3. Vous étudiez les maths.

4. Tu passes des heures à la bibliothèque.
5. Anne et Sophie visitent Paris.

E. Questions personnelles. Answer the questions you hear in complete sentences. Write only your answer, not the question.

1. Est-ce que vous aimez voyager?
2. Allez-vous souvent au supermarché?
3. Est-ce qu'il y a une télévision dans votre chambre?
4. Préférez-vous voyager en avion ou en voiture?
5. Avez-vous des cousins?

Unit Test 3B

A. Des amis. You will hear five statements about various people. If the noun in the sentence is masculine, mark row one: **masculin.** If the noun in the sentence is feminine, mark row two: **féminin.** If it is impossible to tell, mark the third row: **impossible à dire.**

MODELS:

 0. Dominique est française.   You would mark row two for **féminin.**
00. C'est un artiste.   You would mark row one for **masculin.**

1. Claude est réservé(e).
2. Ce sont des ami(e)s sympathiques.
3. Michel(le) est célibataire.

4. Voici une étudiante anglaise.
5. Ce sont des journalistes intelligents.

B. Logique ou illogique? You will hear five pairs of sentences. For each pair, decide whether the second action logically follows the first action, and mark either **logique** or **illogique** on the chart below.

MODEL:

0. Anne va au restaurant. Elle va dîner avec un copain.   You would mark row one for **logique.**

1. Je vais à l'hôpital. Je vais nager.
2. Anne va à la gare. Elle va regarder un film.
3. Henri va au stade. Il va jouer au football avec des copains.
4. Nous allons à l'église. Nous aimons beaucoup voyager.
5. Nicole va à la bibliothèque. Elle va étudier.

C. Une chambre d'étudiant(e). Answer the following questions affirmatively or negatively according to the picture below.

MODEL:

0. Est-ce qu'il y a des livres?   You would mark: **Oui, il y a des livres.**

1. Est-ce qu'il y a des cassettes?
2. Est-ce qu'il y a un appareil-photo?
3. Est-ce qu'il y a un vélo?

4. Est-ce qu'il y a un ordinateur?
5. Est-ce qu'il y a une radio?

D. Demain aussi. Listen to what the following people are doing. Then say that tomorrow they are going to do the same things.

MODEL:

0. Je travaille.   You would write: **Demain aussi, je vais travailler.**

1. Tu passes chez Marc.
2. Éric joue du piano.
3. Mes amis voyagent en train.

4. Nous restons chez nous.
5. Vous jouez aux cartes.

E. Questions personnelles. Answer the questions you hear in complete sentences. Write only your answer, not the question.

1. Est-ce que vous aimez la musique?
2. Avez-vous un camarade de chambre?
3. Est-ce que vous avez un vélo?
4. Est-ce que vous allez à la bibliothèque à pied ou à vélo?
5. À Thanksgiving, comment est-ce que vous rentrez chez vous? en bus? en voiture? en avion?

Unit Test 4A

A. Le budget de Dominique. You will hear about Dominique's budget. Fill in the amounts of her expenses or income for each item.

Dominique habite un studio avec deux camarades. Le loyer est de 365 euros par mois.
Pour les transports, Dominique dépense 39 euros par mois.
Pour les loisirs, en général, elle dépense 164 euros par mois.
Elle a une petite bourse de 172 euros par mois.
Pour le téléphone, elle et ses camarades dépensent 27 euros par mois.

B. Dans la maison. You will hear four sentences describing what the six members of the Boudin family are doing. Then indicate which room they are probably in by choosing the appropriate letter.

MODEL:

0. Médor Boudin (*the family dog*) joue avec Michel et Marc. Médor est dans _____.

    (a) le jardin   (b) la salle à manger   (c) le salon

    You would choose (a) for **le jardin.**

1. Michel et Marc Boudin font la vaisselle.
2. Grand-mère Boudin regarde un programme à la télévision avec ses amis.
3. Monsieur et Madame Boudin vont dîner.
4. Marie Boudin étudie sur son lit.

C. Une question de culture. You will hear five statements about French culture. Listen carefully and decide whether each statement is true (**vrai**) or false (**faux**).

MODEL:

0: Paris est la capitale de la France.   You would mark **vrai.**

1. Beaucoup de Français utilisent des services en ligne pour gérer leurs comptes bancaires.
2. En France, les études universitaires coûtent très cher.
3. En France, un grand nombre d'étudiants ont des bourses.
4. Pour les étudiants français, il est facile de trouver un logement bon marché.
5. En France, le shopping est une forme de récréation.

D. Possessions. We all like to brag. Listen carefully to the following people bragging about their possessions and then complete the sentences below with the appropriate possessive adjectives.

MODELS:

0. J'ai un joli appartement.   You would mark **mon** in the blank.
   Tu as de nouveaux meubles.   You would mark **tes** in the blank.

1. Nous avons une nouvelle maison.   4. Nathalie a un beau tailleur.
2. Vous avez des chaussures noires.   5. Tu as une belle cravate.
3. Mes cousins ont un grand studio à Paris.   6. Pierre a un vieux jean américain.

E. Activités. Listen to the things these procrastinators plan on doing in the future. Imagine that they decide to do these things right away and express what they're doing in the present tense, according to the model.

MODEL:

0. Je vais chercher un appartement.   You would write: **Je cherche un appartement.**

1. Nous allons faire des économies.   4. Tu vas payer le loyer.
2. Mes sœurs vont nettoyer leur chambre.   5. Vous allez faire une promenade.
3. Sophie va acheter un anorak.

F. Comparaisons personnelles. Listen to each question carefully and then express your opinion with a complete sentence.

1. Parlons des transports. Est-ce qu'une voiture est plus chère ou moins chère qu'un vélo?
2. Maintenant, parlons de vous. Êtes-vous plus jeune ou moins jeune que votre meilleur(e) ami(e)?
3. Finalement, parlons de chez vous. Quelle est la pièce la plus confortable?

Unit Test 4B

A. Le budget d'Isabelle. You will hear about Isabelle's budget. Fill in the amounts of her expenses or income for each item.

Isabelle habite un appartement dans le Quartier latin avec deux copines.
Le loyer est de 546 euros par mois.
Elle est très chic; alors elle dépense 182 euros par mois pour les vêtements.
Elle adore aller au restaurant. Pour ses repas, elle dépense 65 euros par mois.
Elle utilise souvent l'Internet et elle dépense 30 euros par mois pour son service Internet.
Au travail, Isabelle fait des sites Internet et gagne 2.286 euros par mois.

B. Dans la maison. You will hear four sentences describing what five members of the Boudin family are doing. Then indicate which room they are probably in by choosing the appropriate letter.

MODEL:

0. Médor Boudin *(the family dog)* joue avec Marie et Marc. Médor est dans _____.

    (a) le jardin   (b) la salle à manger   (c) le salon

    You would choose (a) for **le jardin.**

1. Monsieur Boudin prépare le dîner.
2. Madame Boudin dîne.
3. Michel Boudin écoute un CD sur son lit.
4. Marie et Marc Boudin regardent un match de football à la télé.

C. Une question de culture. You will hear five statements about French culture. Listen carefully and decide whether each statement is true **(vrai)** or false **(faux).**

MODEL:

0. Paris est la capitale de la France.   You would mark **vrai.**

1. En France, on ne paie pratiquement pas de frais de scolarité.
2. Beaucoup de Français visitent des sites marchands sur le Net pour faire leur shopping en ligne.
3. En France, un petit nombre d'étudiants a des bourses.
4. Le Quartier latin est le quartier le plus calme de Paris.
5. Si on est étudiant à Paris, la meilleure solution au problème du logement est d'avoir une chambre à la Cité Universitaire.

D. Possessions. We all like to brag. Listen carefully to the following people bragging about their possessions and then complete the sentences below with the appropriate possessive adjectives.

MODELS:

  0. J'ai un joli appartement.   You would mark **mon** in the blank.
00. Tu as de nouveaux meubles.   You would mark **tes** in the blank.

1. Mes parents ont une belle chambre.   4. Tu as un nouveau pantalon.
2. Vous avez un beau jardin.   5. Olivier a un joli pull bleu.
3. Carole a des lunettes de soleil noires.

E. Activités. Listen to the things these procrastinators plan on doing in the future. Imagine that they decide to do these things right away and express what they are doing in the present tense, according to the model.

MODEL:

0. Je vais chercher un appartement.   You would write: **Je cherche un appartement.**

1. Nous allons gagner de l'argent.   4. Tu vas acheter un ordinateur.
2. Mes frères vont faire leurs devoirs.   5. Vous allez louer une maison à Nice.
3. Monique va répéter sa leçon.

F. Comparaisons personnelles. Listen to each question carefully and then express your opinion with a complete sentence.

1. Parlons du logement. Est-ce qu'un appartement est plus cher ou moins cher qu'une maison?
2. Parlons de l'argent. Dépensez-vous plus ou moins que votre camarade de chambre?
3. Parlons des saisons. Quelle est la meilleure saison?

        Testing Program **TP** **9**

Unit Test 5A

A. Dates historiques. You will hear five statements about important events in French history. Write the dates in the blanks.

MODEL:

0. Guillaume le Conquérant a gagné la Bataille de Hastings en 1066.   You would write **1066.**

1. Jeanne d'Arc a délivré Orléans en 1429.
2. En 1804, Napoléon est devenu empereur.
3. En 1793, Marie-Antoinette a été guillotinée.
4. Philippe-Auguste est mort en 1223.
5. Henri IV a été assassiné en 1610.

B. Voyage au présent ou voyage au passé? You will hear six statements. Some refer to a trip that is currently taking place. Others refer to a trip that took place sometime last year. Listen carefully to the verb. If the verb is in the present tense, mark row one: **présent.** If the verb is in the passé composé, mark row two: **passé composé.**

MODELS:

0. Nous sommes à Paris.   You would mark row one for **présent.**
00. Nous avons été à Québec.   You would mark row two for **passé composé.**

1. Claude est parti avec ses copains.
2. Nous sommes allé(e)s en Normandie.
3. Tu as oublié ton appareil-photo.
4. Vous êtes à Toulouse.
5. Je visite le Louvre.
6. Mes cousins ont fait un séjour à Genève.

C. Combien? You will hear five statements about various people. If the subject of the sentence is singular, mark row one: **singulier.** If the subject of the sentence is plural, mark row two: **pluriel.**

MODELS:

0. Il réussit à l'examen.   You would mark row one for **singulier.**
00. Elles ne réussissent pas à l'examen.   You would mark row two for **pluriel.**

1. Elles rendent visite à Madame Duroc.
2. Il sort ce soir.
3. Elle vend son vélo.
4. Il choisit un chapeau rouge.
5. Ils ne dorment pas.

D. Une question de culture. You will hear five statements about different aspects of French culture. Indicate whether they are true (**vrai**) or false (**faux**).

MODEL:

0. Paris est la capitale de la France.   You would mark row one for **vrai.**

1. Les Français ne font pas attention à leur santé.
2. Il n'y a pas beaucoup d'étudiants étrangers en France.
3. Paris est le centre politique, économique et culturel de la France.
4. Il y a beaucoup d'étudiants américains en France.
5. En France, peu d'étudiants étrangers sont d'origine française.

E. Hier aussi. Listen to what is happening and/or what the following people are doing. Then say that yesterday the same things happened. Use the **passé composé.**

MODEL:

0. Paul joue au tennis.   You would write: **Hier aussi, il a joué au tennis.**

1. Sophie attend ses copains.
2. Nous rencontrons nos amis.
3. Il pleut.
4. Vous partez après le dîner.
5. Tu fais une promenade.
6. Marc et Pierre restent chez eux.
7. Je réussis à l'examen.

Unit Test 5B

A. Dates historiques. You will hear five statements about important events in French history. Write the dates in the blanks.

MODEL:

0. François 1ᵉʳ est né en 1494.   You would write **1494.**

1. Guillaume le Conquérant a gagné la Bataille de Hastings en <u>1066</u>.
2. En <u>1431</u>, Jeanne d'Arc est morte brûlée vive (*burned alive*).
3. Le 14 juillet <u>1789</u>, la Révolution française a commencé.
4. La Deuxième Guerre mondiale a fini en <u>1945</u>.
5. En janvier de l'an <u>2002</u>, l'Europe va adopter l'euro.

B. Voyage au présent ou voyage au passé? You will hear six statements. Some refer to a trip that is currently taking place. Others refer to a trip that took place sometime last year. Listen carefully to the verb. If the verb is in the present tense, mark row one: **présent.** If the verb is in the passé composé, mark row two: **passé composé.**

MODELS:

  0. Vous êtes à Montréal.   You would mark row one for **présent.**
00. Vous avez visité la ville de Québec.   You would mark row two for **passé composé.**

1. Manon a eu peur.
2. Ils ne maigrissent pas à Noël.
3. Tu as choisi un IBM.
4. Nous sommes arrivés à trois heures.
5. J'ai fait la connaissance de ma copine en vacances.
6. Ils sortent tous les week-ends.

C. Combien? You will hear five statements about various people. If the subject of the sentence is singular, mark row one: **singulier.** If the subject of the sentence is plural, mark row two: **pluriel.**

MODELS:

  0. Elle ne part pas demain.   You would mark row one for **singulier.**
00. Ils ne partent pas après l'examen.   You would mark row two for **pluriel.**

1. Elle ne vend pas son VTT.
2. Il dort beaucoup.
3. Ils finissent à 4 heures.
4. Elle réussit aux examens.
5. Ils répondent souvent en classe.

D. Une question de culture. You will hear five statements about different aspects of French culture. Indicate whether they are true (**vrai**) or false (**faux**).

MODEL:

0. La Tour Eiffel est à Paris.   You would mark row one for **vrai.**

1. La santé est une chose très importante pour les Français.
2. En France, beaucoup d'étudiants étrangers viennent d'Afrique.
3. À Paris, il n'y a pas d'architecture très moderne.
4. Paris n'est pas une ville moderne.
5. ERASMUS est un programme d'échange européen.

E. Hier aussi. Listen to what is happening and/or what the following people are doing. Then say that yesterday the same things happened. Use the **passé composé.**

MODEL:

0. Julie visite Rome.   You would write: **Hier aussi, elle a visité Rome.**

1. Sophie a sommeil.
2. Arthur et André dorment bien.
3. Il neige.
4. Vous faites la connaissance de quelqu'un.
5. Les étudiants vont au cinéma.
6. J'attends le bus.
7. Nous perdons notre temps.

Unit Test 6A

A. Combien? You will hear five statements about various people. If the subject of the sentence is singular, mark row one: **singulier.** If the subject of the sentence is plural, mark row two: **pluriel.**

Models:

0. Il fait les courses.   You would mark row one for **singulier.**
00. Elles ne font pas la cuisine.   You would mark row two for **pluriel.**

1. Ils ne font pas de sport.   4. Elles boivent du thé.
2. Ils prennent du café.   5. Elle met la table.
3. Il comprend la leçon.

B. Présent ou passé? You will hear five statements. Listen carefully. If the verb is in the present tense, mark row one: **présent.** If the verb is in the passé composé, mark row two: **passé composé.**

Models:

0. Nous servons de la tarte aux pommes.   You would mark row one for **présent.**
00. Ils ont servi du café après le repas.   You would mark row two for **passé composé.**

1. Nous avons bu de la limonade.   4. Je prends du saumon, s'il vous plaît.
2. J'ai compris la question après.   5. Mettez-vous du poivre sur votre steak?
3. Elle est revenue de Paris ce matin.

C. Vrai ou faux? You will hear six statements. Indicate whether each one is true **(vrai)** or false **(faux).**

Model:

0. Le poulet est une sorte de poisson.   You would mark row two for **faux.**

1. Les hôtels français en ligne ne réussissent pas très bien.
2. Les Français mangent beaucoup au petit déjeuner.
3. Beaucoup de Français mangent plus à midi que les Américains.
4. Les cerises et les poires sont des légumes.
5. On met souvent du sucre dans le café.
6. On ne commande pas de bière si on est au régime.

D. Questions personnelles. Answer the questions you hear with complete sentences. Write only your answer (not the question).

1. Qu'est-ce que vous buvez au petit déjeuner?
2. Avez-vous autant d'argent ou moins d'argent que vos copains?
3. Avez-vous trop de travail ou peu de travail pour la classe de français?
4. Avez-vous déjà voyagé en Europe?

Unit Test 6B

A. Combien? You will hear five statements about various people. If the subject of the sentence is singular, mark row one: **singulier.** If the subject of the sentence is plural, mark row two: **pluriel.**

Models:

0. Elle comprend l'espagnol.   You would mark row one for **singulier.**
00. Elles ne comprennent pas le chinois. You would mark row two for **pluriel.**

1. Elle prend du café le matin.   4. Ils boivent du vin rouge.
2. Ils mettent du beurre sur les croissants! 5. Elle vient de la Martinique.
3. Ils ne font pas de gym.

B. Présent ou passé? You will hear five statements. Listen carefully. If the verb is in the present tense, mark row one: **présent.** If the verb is in the passé composé, mark row two: **passé composé.**

MODELS:

0. Nous commandons un sandwich.   You would mark row one for **présent.**
00. Ils ont servi le café après le repas.   You would mark row two for **passé composé.**

1. Je bois du champagne.   4. Gabriel a mis la table.
2. Ils apprennent l'italien à Rome.   5. Nous ne prenons pas de pain.
3. Paul et Sophie n'ont pas pris de dessert.

C. Vrai ou faux? You will hear six statements. Indicate whether each one is true (**vrai**) or false (**faux**).

MODEL:

0. Les Français adorent le sport.   You would mark row one for **vrai.**

1. Il n'est pas possible d'organiser un voyage en France sur le Net.
2. Les jus de fruit sont populaires en France.
3. La nourriture n'est pas très importante pour les Français.
4. Les vins français sont de mauvaise qualité.
5. Tous les Français reviennent à la maison à midi pour le déjeuner.
6. Normalement, le repas du soir est assez simple, chez les Français.

D. Questions personnelles. Answer the questions you hear with complete sentences. Write only your answer (not the question).

1. Buvez-vous du lait avec le dîner?
2. Mangez-vous plus de légumes ou moins de légumes que vos parents?
3. Mangez-vous des fruits tous les jours?
4. Avez-vous déjà voyagé au Mexique?

Unit Test 7A

A. Logique ou illogique? Listen to the five pairs of sentences and decide whether they are logical (**logique**) or illogical (**illogique**).

MODEL:

0. Nous suivons un cours de sciences économiques. Alors nous lisons beaucoup de poèmes.
   You would mark row one for **logique.**

1. Julie n'est pas venue en classe. Alors je vais lui prêter mes notes.
2. Vous avez raté votre examen. Alors vous êtes reçu(e).
3. Il est nécessaire de payer une scolarité. C'est parce que l'université est gratuite.
4. Tu dis toujours la vérité. Alors tu racontes beaucoup de mensonges.
5. Éric n'a pas le temps d'écrire des lettres. Alors il envoie des cartes postales.

B. Les étudiants universitaires. You are going to hear eight sentences about some students at an American university. If the subject of the sentence is singular, mark **singulier.** If the subject of the sentence is plural, mark **pluriel.** If it is impossible to say one way or another, mark **singulier ou pluriel.**

MODELS:

0. Il réussit à l'examen.   You would mark row one for **singulier.**
00. Elles ne réussissent pas à l'examen.   You would mark row two for **pluriel.**
000. Il(s) prépare(nt) les examens très sérieusement. You would mark row three for **singulier ou pluriel.**

1. Elle fait des études de chimie.   5. Ils veulent obtenir un diplôme.
2. Il suit un cours de biologie.   6. Elles lisent un roman espagnol.
3. Elle(s) n'enseigne(nt) pas à l'université.   7. Il doit obtenir de bonnes notes.
4. Il écrit un poème pour le cours d'anglais.   8. Ils ne peuvent pas raconter d'histoires.

C. L'éducation en France. Listen to the following sentences on education in France and indicate whether they are **vrai** (true) or **faux** (false).

MODEL:

0. Le système des diplômes français est différent du système américain.
   You would mark row one for **vrai.**

1. Les étudiants français passent le baccalauréat à 22 ans.
2. Avec le bac, on peut aller directement à l'université.
3. Pour entrer dans une grande école, il faut être reçu à un examen d'entrée difficile.
4. Les études universitaires sont gratuites aux États-Unis.
5. Les étudiants français sont très actifs pour la protection et la défense de leurs droits. .
6. Les étudiants français trouvent qu'il n'y a pas assez de professeurs en France.

D. Questions: la vie à l'université. Answer the following questions. Use object pronouns in your answers.

MODEL:

0. Est-ce que vous aimez vos cours?   You would write: **Oui, je les aime.**

1. Est-ce que vous connaissez le président de l'université?
2. Est-ce que vous trouvez le français difficile?
3. Est-ce que vous comprenez vos camarades?
4. Est-ce que vous regardez souvent la télévision?
5. Est-ce que vous écrivez souvent à vos grands-parents?
6. Est-ce que vos parents vous téléphonent souvent?

Unit Test 7B

A. Logique ou illogique? Listen to the five pairs of sentences and decide whether they are **logique** or **illogique.**

MODEL:

0. Nous suivons un cours de sciences économiques. Alors nous lisons beaucoup de poèmes.
   You would mark row two for **illogique.**

1. Julie a eu une bonne note à l'examen. Alors elle a réussi à l'examen.
2. Nous passons un examen. Alors nous sommes reçus.
3. J'ai suivi un cours de philosophie. Je comprends la philosophie.
4. Tu veux être écrivain. Tu étudies la littérature.
5. Ils doivent rester à la maison. Ils veulent voir un film au cinéma.

B. Les étudiants universitaires. You are going to hear eight sentences about some students at an American university. If the subject of the sentence is singular, mark **singulier.** If the subject of the sentence is plural, mark **pluriel.** If it is impossible to say one way or another, mark **singulier ou pluriel.**

MODELS:

  0. Il réussit à l'examen.   You would mark row one for **singulier.**
 00. Elles ne réussissent pas à l'examen.   You would mark row two for **pluriel.**
000. Il(s) prépare(nt) les examens très sérieusement.   You would mark row three for **singulier ou pluriel.**

1. Elles font des recherches sur le cancer.
2. Ils ont suivi des cours de marketing.
3. Il dit toujours la vérité.
4. Elles passe(nt) l'examen.
5. Elles connaissent plusieurs acteurs.
6. Elle décrit l'accident.
7. Il(s) prépare(nt) l'examen de maths.
8. Il doit étudier ce soir.

C. L'éducation en France. Listen to the following phrases on education in France and indicate whether they are **vrai** (true) or **faux** (false).

MODEL:

0. Il n'y a pas de différences entre les universités françaises et américaines.
   You would mark row two for **faux.**

1. Les études secondaires sont gratuites aux États-Unis.
2. Les étudiants français passent le bac à 18 ans.
3. Tous les étudiants qui passent le bac réussissent.
4. Avec le bac on peut entrer dans une grande école.
5. Moins d'étudiants font des études supérieures en France qu'aux U.S.A.
6. Les étudiants français ne participent pas souvent à des manifestations.

D. Questions: la vie à l'université. Answer the following questions. Use object pronouns in your answers.

MODEL:

0. Est-ce que vous aimez vos camarades de classe?   You would write: **Oui, je les aime.**

1. Est-ce que vous aimez la télévision?
2. Est-ce que vos professeurs vous aiment bien?
3. Est-ce que vous apprenez l'espagnol?
4. Est-ce que vous posez des questions à votre professeur?
5. Est-ce que vous téléphonez souvent à vos parents?
6. Est-ce que votre copain vous écrit des poèmes?

Unit Test 8A

A. Passé composé ou imparfait? You will hear five sentences. Listen to them carefully and then decide if each sentence is in the **passé composé** or the **imparfait.**

MODELS:

 0. Dimanche, je suis allé au cinéma.   You would mark row one for **passé composé.**
00. Il y avait beaucoup d'étudiants au cinéma.   You would mark row two for **imparfait.**

1. En 1984, nous vivions à Paris.
2. Mes parents avaient un appartement dans le Quartier latin.
3. Un jour quelque chose de bizarre est arrivé.
4. Il y a eu un cambriolage chez nous.
5. Les cambrioleurs sont partis tout de suite!

B. La vie en France. Listen to the following sentences on French culture. Listen carefully and then decide if each sentence is **vrai** (true) or **faux** (false).

MODEL:

0. Les Français ne regardent pas beaucoup de télévision.   You would mark row two for **faux.**

1. Aujourd'hui 80 pour cent des Français habitent dans des villes.
2. Lyon est la plus ancienne ville française.
3. Il est possible de voir des feuilletons américains à la télévision en France.
4. Aujourd'hui toutes les chaînes de télévision sont privées.
5. Un gendarme fait le même travail qu'un agent de police.
6. Un département est une division culturelle du territoire français.

C. Autrefois. Everyone likes to remember the "good old days." Answer the following questions about your childhood in complete sentences.

1. Habitiez-vous en banlieue quand vous étiez petit(e)?
2. Parliez-vous une autre langue?
3. Quel était votre dessin animé favori?
4. Lisiez-vous beaucoup quand vous étiez petit(e)?

Unit Test 8B

A. Passé composé ou imparfait? You will hear five sentences. Listen to them carefully and then decide if each sentence is in the **passé composé** or the **imparfait.**

MODELS:

  0. Dimanche, je suis allé(e) au cinéma.   You would mark row one for **passé composé.**
00. Il y avait beaucoup d'étudiants au cinéma.   You would mark row two for **imparfait.**

1. Nous avons pris le bus pour aller en ville.   4. Normalement on prenait le métro.
2. En 1980, est-ce que vous travailliez à New York?   5. Mes amis ont vécu plusieurs années à Boston.
3. Où vivais-tu l'année dernière?

B. La vie en France. Listen to the following sentences on French culture. Listen carefully and then decide if each sentence is **vrai** (true) or **faux** (false).

MODEL:

0. Les Français ne regardent pas beaucoup de télévision.   You would mark row two for **faux.**

1. En 1900, 80 pour cent des Français habitaient dans des villes.
2. La ville de Strasbourg est située sur le Rhin.
3. Canal Plus est une chaîne de télévision française.
4. La vidéo sur Internet n'a pas d'influence sur la télévision traditionnelle.
5. La France est divisée en 95 départements.
6. Le guarde républicain assure la sécurité du Président de la République.

C. Autrefois. Everyone likes to remember the "good old days." Answer the following questions about your childhood in complete sentences.

1. Regardiez-vous souvent la télévision?   3. Où habitiez-vous quand vous aviez cinq ans?
2. Quel était votre feuilleton favori?   4. Partiez-vous souvent en vacances?

Unit Test 9A

A. Singulier ou pluriel? You will hear seven statements. Mark row one if the subject of the sentence is **singulier.** Mark row two if the subject of the sentence is **pluriel.** Mark row three if the subject of the sentence could be **singulier ou pluriel.**

MODELS:

  0. Il(s) se disputent souvent.   You would mark **singulier ou pluriel.**
00. Il ouvre le magasin à 7h.   You would mark **singulier.**

1. Elles sont en forme.   5. Ils ont rendez-vous à 20h.
2. Il(s) pratique(nt) l'alpinisme.   6. Elle(s) se lave(nt) les cheveux tous les jours.
3. Elle(s) se réveille(nt) à 7h.   7. Elles en ont dix.
4. Il prend toujours une douche le matin.

B. La vie en France. You will hear six statements about French culture. Mark whether each statement is true (**vrai**) or false (**faux**).

MODEL:

0. L'activité la plus populaire en France est la télévision.   You would mark **vrai.**

1. Les Français ont souvent des difficultés à occuper leur temps libre.
2. Les HLM sont une innovation sociale importante.
3. Les HLM sont toujours situées près des parcs.
4. Les jeunes Français se rencontrent souvent dans des boums ou dans des fêtes privées.
5. Dans une soirée, les invités sont toujours bien habillés.
6. Pour s'amuser dans une fête, les jeunes Français aiment regarder la télévision.

C. Activités. Listen to what the following people have with them, and then say what they are doing, using an appropriate reflexive construction.

MODEL:

0. J'ai du dentifrice.   You would write: **Je me brosse les dents.**

1. Tu as un chemisier et un jean.   3. Elle a des chaussures confortables.
2. Ils ont une brosse.   4. Nous avons un rasoir.

D. Suggestions et conseils. Tell the following people to do certain things. Use the **tu** or **vous** form, according to the context.

MODEL:

0. Dites à Pierre et Paul de se coucher.   You would write: **Couchez-vous!**

1. Dites à Fatima de s'habiller.   3. Dites à Simon de s'excuser.
2. Dites à Sophie et Denis de ne pas s'énerver.   4. Dites à Olivier de ne pas se tromper.

Unit Test 9B

A. Singulier ou pluriel? You will hear seven statements. Mark row one if the subject of the sentence is **singulier.** Mark row two is the subject of the sentence is **pluriel.** Mark row three if the subject of the sentence could be **singulier ou pluriel.**

MODELS:

 0. Il(s) se lave(nt) dans la salle de bains.   You would mark **singulier ou pluriel.**
00. Ils font de la voile.   You would mark **pluriel.**

1. Il a l'air fatigué.   5. Ils ouvrent la porte du garage.
2. Elle(s) s'achète(nt) des chaussures.   6. Ils s'entendent bien.
3. Ils ont mal au cœur.   7. Ils y vont demain.
4. Elle est en mauvaise santé.

B. La vie en France. You will hear six statements about French culture. Mark whether each statement is true (**vrai**) or false (**faux**).

MODEL:

0. Les français regardent beaucoup la télévision.   You would mark **vrai.**

1. Vingt millions de Français sont connectés au Net.
2. La majorité des Français qui habitent les grandes villes vivent en appartement.
3. Les HLM ou habitations à loyer modéré ne sont pas modernes.
4. Une soirée est plus sophistiquée et formelle qu'une fête.
5. Dans les fêtes, les jeunes Français aiment boire de la bière et dormir.
6. Aujourd'hui il y a des écoles et des lycées mixtes en France.

C. Activités. Listen to what the following people have with them, and then say what they are doing, using an appropriate reflexive construction.

MODEL:

0. Monique a une jupe et un pull.   You would write: **Elle s'habille.**

1. J'ai une brosse à dents.
2. Nous avons du savon.

3. Tu as un rasoir.
4. Vous avez un peigne.

D. Suggestions et conseils. Tell the following people to do certain things. Use the **tu** or **vous** form, according to the context.

MODEL:

0. Dites à Monique de faire des exercices.   You would write: **Fais des exercices.**

1. Dites à François de se reposer.
2. Dites à vos amis Pierre et Anne de se dépêcher.
3. Dites à Éric de s'asseoir.
4. Dites à Claire et Monique de ne pas se lever.

Unit Test 10A

A. La rencontre. A mutual friend, Véronique Fournier, decides to introduce Pierre and Chantal to one another because they have a lot in common and she thinks they will get along well. Listen to the story of how they meet and fill in the blanks with the word you hear.

Véronique a donné rendez-vous à Pierre pour 4h au café parisien La Coupole. Elle lui a dit qu'elle a une amie qui vient avec elle. Pierre arrive <u>ponctuellement</u> à 4h et cherche partout mais Véronique et son amie ne sont pas là. Il s'assied, commande un café crème et il les attend <u>patiemment</u>. Enfin, à 4h30 les deux filles arrivent. Véronique s'excuse et elle explique qu' <u>évidemment</u>, elles avaient raté leur bus. Pierre lui répond <u>gentiment</u> que ça va. Alors, Véronique les présente l'un à l'autre et tout le monde s'assied. Véronique commence à parler <u>brillamment</u> d'un film qu'elle vient de voir mais les deux autres sont timides et ils ne disent rien. Mais quand Véronique dit une bêtise (*something stupid*) au sujet du film, Chantal, qui est une grande cinéphile, commence à donner ses opinions personnelles. Elle discute <u>sérieusement</u> de la cinématographie. Pierre l'écoute <u>poliment</u> et il commence, alors, à s'intéresser à cette fille intelligente.

B. La vie en France. Pierre et Chantal are typically French in their opinions about marriage, careers, mobility, and vacations. Based upon your knowledge of French customs and attitudes found in the *Notes culturelles*, indicate whether the following statements are **vrai** or **faux**.

MODEL:

0. Les Français se marient relativement tard.   You would mark **vrai**.

1. En France, il faut se marier d'abord à la mairie.
2. Le gouvernement français ne reconnaît pas officiellement l'union libre.
3. Les Français travaillent moins d'heures par semaine aujourd'hui que dans le passé.
4. Il y a très peu de chômage en France.
5. Pour les Français, les vacances sont sacrées.
6. Les Français ont deux semaines de congés payés en été.

C. L'immeuble de Chantal. Pierre stops by Chantal's apartment building and notices the mailboxes. As you hear each apartment number, fill in the corresponding floor on your answer sheet. For example, apartment 328 would be on the third floor.

MODEL:

0. Les Neis habitent au 728.   You would write: **Les Neis habitent au septième étage.**

1. Les Fabre habitent au 210.
2. Chantal habite au 480.
3. Les Guérin habitent au 123.

4. Les Saint Martin habitent au 850.
5. Les Verdier habitent au 508.
6. Les Perez habitent au 329.

Unit Test 10B

A. La cérémonie. The groom and all the guests have already arrived at the town hall and are anxiously awaiting the bride-to-be. **Les témoins** (*the witnesses*) and **le maire** (*the mayor*) are there as well. Listen to find out what happened before the ceremony began. Fill in the blanks with the word you hear.

Marc est arrivé en avance comme d'habitude et <u>malheureusement</u>, Élodie est en retard. Marc est très déçu. Pourtant, la cérémonie doit commencer dans un instant. Marc regarde sa montre <u>constamment</u>. Il lui avait bien dit 16h, il se dit <u>calmement</u>. À 16h15, il commence à s'inquiéter. Il se demande <u>sérieusement</u> si Élodie n'a pas changé d'avis. Elle lui avait dit plusieurs fois qu'elle voulait <u>vraiment</u> passer le reste de sa vie avec lui. Mais depuis deux semaines elle parle constamment de son nouveau voisin, Bob. Bob est américain. C'est un bel homme sportif qui passe six mois aux États-Unis et six mois en France. Marc a remarqué que quand Bob parle, elle l'écoute toujours très <u>attentivement</u>. Est-ce l'amour ou <u>seulement</u> son joli accent américain qu'elle apprécie? Mais <u>finalement</u> Marc aperçoit la mariée qui arrive. Elle le regarde <u>longuement</u> et <u>amoureusement</u>. La cérémonie peut commencer.

B. La vie en France. Élodie and Marc are typically French in their opinions about marriage, careers, mobility, and vacations. Based upon your knowledge of French customs and attitudes found in the **Notes culturelles,** indicate whether the following statements are **vrai** or **faux.**

MODEL:

0. En France, on passe toute sa vie au même endroit.   You would mark **faux.**

1. Aujourd'hui beaucoup de couples vivent en union libre, sans être mariés.
2. Le mariage est toujours célébré à la mairie d'abord.
3. En France, tout le monde est obligé de travailler 40 heures par semaine.
4. La Sécurité Sociale donne une bonne protection sociale.
5. En été, peu de gens partent en vacances en France.
6. Pour les vacances, les Français adorent la mer et la montagne.

C. Les faire-part. (*The Invitations*). Several weeks before the wedding, Élodie and Marc prepare the invitations to be mailed. All of their friends live in Paris, but in different **arrondissements.** The last two digits of each zip code indicate **l'arrondissement.** Listen to the zip code and then write which **arrondissement** they live in.

MODEL:

0. Les Laforgue - 75014   You would write: **Les Laforgue habitent dans le quatorzième arrondissement.**

1. Les Fabre - 75011
2. Chantal et Robert Saïd - 75001
3. Michel Martin - 75003
4. Les Saintonge - 75016
5. Isabelle et Jacques Van Mol - 75008
6. Marie-Pierre Bouchez - 75019

Unit Test 11A

A. Avant de partir. Madame Javert and her husband, Jean, live in Vermont and are traveling to Québec this summer. She is a worrier and he is very demanding. Listen to the message she left on her best friend's answering machine and fill in the blanks with the verb that you hear.

Salut, Sophie! C'est Andrée. Je ne sais pas quoi faire! Il faut que je <u>fasse</u> tellement de choses avant de partir en vacances. D'abord mon mari veut que je <u>prenne</u> des places sur un vol d'Air Canada. Bien sûr, il faut que ces places <u>soient</u> bon marché! Donc, il faut que j'<u>aille</u> chez l'agent de voyage ou peut-être que je trouverais ça sur Internet. Qui sait? Il est aussi essentiel que nous <u>soyons</u> logés dans un hôtel moderne. Il est nécessaire que notre hôtel <u>ait</u> tous les conforts! En plus, il est possible que notre chat, Einstein, <u>vienne</u> avec nous. Alors, il est essentiel que nous <u>puissions</u> trouver un hôtel qui accepte les animaux. Il n'est pas sûr qu'on en trouve un. Et puis, je ne pense pas que nous <u>ayons</u> besoin de nos passeports. Sais-tu si on en a besoin? Je veux que tu me <u>rappelles</u> tout de suite pour me donner des conseils! À bientôt!

B. Les Québécois, les Européens et la technologie. Listen to the following statements regarding Québec, Europe, and technology in France, and decide whether they are **vrai** or **faux.**

MODEL:

0. Tous les Canadiens sont francophones.   You would mark **faux.**

1. Si on habite aux États-Unis, il est moins cher d'aller au Québec qu'en France.
2. Il n'y a pas de différence entre le français parlé au Québec et le français qu'on parle en France.
3. En 2001, l'euro devient la monnaie courante dans les pays de l'Union européenne.
4. Le Traité de Rome a créé la Communauté économique européenne.
5. L'Espagne et le Portugal ne sont pas encore membres de l'Union européenne.
6. La compagnie Airbus Industrie est un des premiers fabricants d'avions civils dans le monde.
7. Il y a maintenant plus de 6 millions d'internautes en France.

C. Au contraire! Michel has strong opinions about everything, as do you. Listen to his ideas and then write the opposite, beginning your sentences with the expressions below.

1. Les Européens sont indépendants.
2. Les universités américaines ont beaucoup d'argent.
3. Il y a trop de violence au cinéma.
4. Les Américains travaillent trop.

D. Questions personnelles. You will hear five questions. Listen to them carefully and then answer them in complete sentences. Write only the answer.

1. Combien de langues parlez-vous?
2. Est-il possible que vous votiez aux prochaines élections présidentielles?
3. Est-ce qu'il est indispensable qu'on respecte les minorités?
4. Croyez-vous à l'horoscope?
5. Croyez-vous que vos parents sont intelligents?

Unit Test 11B

A. Vive la France profonde! Your French grandfather is not in favor of the European Union; his father fought in World War II. He left this message on your answering machine because he thinks there is hope for you yet. Listen to the message and fill in the blanks with the missing verb that you hear.

Bonjour, Laure. Comment vas-tu? C'est Pépé. Il faut que je te parle. J'ai peur qu'on <u>perde</u> notre identité française. Il est préférable que nous <u>quittions</u> l'Union européenne pour qu'on <u>retrouve</u> nos bonnes traditions. Je doute qu'on <u>puisse</u> se sentir français et européen. En plus, il n'est pas vrai que tout le monde <u>veuille</u> une monnaie unique. Je sais que l'Allemagne et l'Angleterre sont nos alliées à l'heure actuelle, mais je déplore qu'elles <u>aient</u> autant d'influence sur notre beau pays. Il faut absolument qu'on <u>fasse</u> quelque chose avant qu'il <u>soit</u> trop tard! Crois-tu que la France <u>comprenne</u> les risques de sa politique européenne? Moi, je n'en suis pas très sûr. Rappelle-moi vite, ma belle, pour continuer cette discussion importante.

B. Les Québécois, les Européens et la technologie. Listen to the following statements regarding Québec, Europe, and technology in France, and decide whether they are **vrai** or **faux.**

MODEL:

0. Tous les Canadiens sont francophones.   You would mark **faux.**

1. Le français parlé au Québec n'est pas très influencé par l'anglais.
2. Beaucoup de Québécois veulent que le Québec se sépare du Canada.
3. L'Angleterre ne participe pas à l'euro.
4. La Suède, l'Autriche et la Finlande ne sont pas encore membres de l'Union européenne.
5. La Communauté européenne est un énorme marché à l'intérieur de l'Europe.
6. Le TGV est un avion français supersonique.
7. On a créé le Minitel en France bien avant la création d'Internet.

TEST SHEETS

Unit Test 1A

A. Qui est-ce? You work at the reception desk of the Hôtel Ritz. You are on the phone and must complete the list of celebrity guests you hear. Each last name will be spelled out for you twice. (18 points)

1. Luc _____   4. Gérard _____

2. Patrick _____   5. Virginie _____

3. Sandrine _____   6. Juliette _____

B. Une lettre. You will hear a letter Moustafa is writing to his American penpal. As you see, the letter is incomplete. Fill in the missing words and/or phrases by listening to the tape. (20 points: 1 point per word)

Cher John,

Salut! Comment _____ _____? Je _____ _____ _____ _____

_____. J'habite *(I live)* à _____, mais je ne suis pas _____. Je suis

_____. J'_____ _____ la musique _____,

mais je _____ le raï parce que c'est une musique _____.

Je _____ _____ tellement les films romantiques. Je _____ le Front national.

Et toi?

_____ _____!

Amitiés,

Moustafa

C. Bonjour! You are going to hear part of a conversation. Write what you hear on the line marked "A" and then complete the conversation with expressions from Unit 1 on line "B." (16 points)

1. A) _____

    B) _____

2. A) _____

    B) _____

3. A) _____

    B) _____

4. A) _____

    B) _____

D. Et vous? Now a little about you. Complete the following sentences describing yourself. (12 points)

1. Je suis _____. (your nationality)

2. Aujourd'hui ça va _____. (mood)

3. J'adore _____. (an actor)

4. Je n'aime pas tellement _____. (an actress)

5. Je déteste _____. (a musical group)

6. Je préfère _____. (a city)

E. Une question de nationalité. Provide the appropriate adjective to describe the following public figures. (8 points)

1. Gérard Depardieu. Il est _____.

2. Céline Dion. Elle est _____.

3. Le Prince William *(Diana's son)*. Il est _____.

4. Oprah Winfrey. Elle est _____.

F. Géographie. Name four places that are part of **la France d'outre-mer.** (8 points)

1. _____   3. _____

2. _____   4. _____

G. Aperçu culturel: Vrai ou faux. Read the following statements. Write (V) for **vrai** if you think the statement is true and (F) for **faux** if you think the statement is false. (20 points)

_____ 1. France is often called **l'Hexagone** because of its shape.

_____ 2. **L'Union européenne** consists of 15 countries.

_____ 3. American culture is virtually unknown in France.

_____ 4. France has very few foreigners.

_____ 5. **Le créole,** a mix of French and African dialects, is spoken in Saint-Pierre-et-Miquelon.

_____ 6. Most recent immigrants to France are from North Africa.

_____ 7. Members of **le Front national** feel that immigrants enrich French culture and plan to encourage more immigration to France.

_____ 8. **Le couscous** is a dish that originated in West Africa.

_____ 9. **L'afro-rock, le raï,** and **le zouk** are new forms of music popular in France.

_____ 10. **M. C. Solaar** has popularized traditional French music throughout the world.

Unit Test 1B

A. Qui est-ce? You work at the reception desk of the Hôtel Ritz. You are on the phone and must complete the list of celebrity guests you hear. Each last name will be spelled out for you. (18 points)

1. Pascale _____

2. Élodie _____

3. Daniel _____

4. Isabelle _____

5. Jean _____

6. Francis _____

B. Une lettre. You will hear a letter Simone is writing to her American penpal. As you see, the letter is incomplete. Fill in the missing words and/or phrases by listening to the tape. (20 points: 1 point per word)

Chère Britney,

Salut! Comment _____-_____? Je _____ _____. J'habite à

_____-_____-_____; c'est à la _____. Je suis

_____. J'_____ la musique _____

et la musique _____. J'_____ _____ les concerts

et le cinéma. Je _____ le cinéma _____. Je _____

_____ tellement le sport. Je _____ la violence et le racisme. Et toi?

À _____.

Bien amicalement,

Simone

C. Bonjour! You're going to hear part of a conversation. Write what you hear on the line marked "A" and then complete the conversation with expressions from Unit 1 on line "B." (16 points)

1. A) _____

   B) _____

2. A) _____

   B) _____

3. A) _____

   B) _____

4. A) _____

   B) _____

D. Et vous? Now a little about you. Complete the following sentences with pertinent information. (12 points)

1. Aujourd'hui je vais _____. (mood)

2. Je suis _____. (your nationality)

3. J'adore _____. (a musical group)

4. Je n'aime pas tellement _____. (a TV show)

5. Je déteste _____. (an actor)

6. Je préfère _____. (a restaurant)

E. Une question de nationalité. Provide the appropriate adjective to describe the following public figures. (8 points)

1. Tony Blair. Il est _____.

2. Hillary Clinton. Elle est _____.

3. Catherine Deneuve. Elle est _____.

4. Michael Jordan. Il est _____.

F. Géographie. Name four places that are part of **la France d'outre-mer.** (8 points)

1. _____   3. _____

2. _____   4. _____

G. Aperçu culturel: Vrai ou faux. Read the following statements. Write (V) for **vrai** if you think the statement is true and (F) for **faux** if you think the statement is false. (20 points)

_____ 1. France is somewhat smaller than Texas in size.

_____ 2. In terms of technology, France is far behind most industrialized countries.

_____ 3. French young people are fascinated by the American way of life and have adopted many of its features.

_____ 4. **Le Minitel** emerged in France as a result of the success of the World Wide Web.

_____ 5. The inhabitants of **la France d'outre-mer** are not French citizens.

_____ 6. Most **Martiniquais** and **Guadeloupéens** are of African origin.

_____ 7. **Les Beurs** are young people who were born in North Africa but live in France.

_____ 8. Members of **le Front national** would like to curtail immigration and repatriate recent immigrants.

_____ 9. **S.O.S. Racisme** is an organization made up of young people who favor a multiethnic society.

_____ 10. **Khaled** plays a type of musique called **raï** and comes from North Africa.

Unit Test 2A

A. Visitons les pays francophones! In Unit 2 we have investigated the Francophone world. You will hear five short descriptions. Listen carefully to the descriptions and then choose the most logical answer. (20 points)

MODEL:

0. Kerlyne habite probablement ____d____.

   (a) en Gaspésie   (b) en Nouvelle Angleterre   (c) en Algérie   (d) en Haïti

1. Lamine habite probablement _____.

   (a) au Québec   (b) en Louisiane   (c) au Sénégal   (d) en Suisse

2. Frédérique étudie probablement _____.

   (a) l'architecture   (b) le français   (c) l'informatique   (d) l'anglais

3. Luc travaille probablement _____.

   (a) à Zurich   (b) à Montréal   (c) à Bruxelles   (d) à Dakar

4. Ahmed habite probablement _____.

   (a) en Belgique   (b) au Maghreb   (c) en Nouvelle Calédonie   (d) au Viêt-nam

5. Claude est probablement _____.

   (a) de France   (b) de la Nouvelle Orléans   (c) du Luxembourg   (d) de Tunisie

B. Quelle heure est-il? Below are six clock faces, each identified by a letter. As you hear each time stated, select the corresponding clock and write the letter on your answer sheet. First, listen to the model. Then write in the letters as you listen to the speaker. (10 points)

MODEL:

0. ____**B.**____

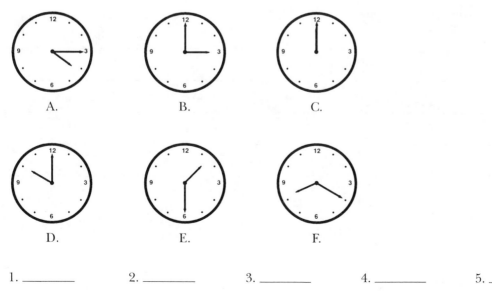

A.   B.   C.

D.   E.   F.

1. _____   2. _____   3. _____   4. _____   5. _____

C. Trois amies. You will hear six statements about the activities of three apartment mates. If all of them are performing the activity, mark the first row: **pluriel.** If only one person is performing the activity, mark the second row: **singulier.** If it is impossible to tell, mark the third row: **impossible à dire.** (12 points)

	0	00	1	2	3	4	5	6
pluriel	✓							
singulier								
impossible à dire		✓						

D. Mathieu. You will hear five sentences about Mathieu, each one containing a number. Listen carefully and write the appropriate numeral in the corresponding blank. (10 points)

MODEL:

0. Il rentre à ____18____ heures.

1. Il ne dîne pas avant _____ heures.

2. Il regarde *Friends* à la télé à _____ heures.

3. Il habite _____, boulevard Saint Michel.

4. Il habite l'appartement numéro _____.

5. Il travaille _____ heures par semaine.

E. La réponse est non! Let's disagree! Listen carefully to each sentence and then write the opposite (the negative form). *Do not* write the affirmative form. (15 points)

MODEL:

0. J'étudie.   You write: **Je n'étudie pas.**

1. _____

2. _____

3. _____

4. _____

5. _____

Copyright © Houghton Mifflin Company. All rights reserved.

F.   Questions personnelles. Your professor finds you fascinating. Answer the following questions in complete sentences so he/she can get to know you. (18 points)

1. _____

2. _____

3. _____

4. _____

5. _____

6. _____

G.   Culture. Read the following statements about Francophone culture. Write (V) for **vrai** if you think the statement is true and (F) for **faux** if you think the statement is false. (15 points)

_____   1.   In **Amérique du Nord** the movement of French settlers began in **Louisiane.**

_____   2.   In 1534 **Saint Laurent** landed in **Gaspésie** and took possession of the area in the name of the king of France.

_____   3.   Samuel Champlain founded the city of **Québec.**

_____   4.   Not many **Québécois** think separation from Canada is a good idea.

_____   5.   **Le Grand Dérangement** was the forced exile of French settlers from Nova Scotia.

_____   6.   In the U.S. **les Créoles** are African-Americans who have come into contact with Cajun culture and the French language.

_____   7.   **Le créole** is the official language of **Haïti.**

_____   8.   The name **Haïti** is Native American in origin.

_____   9.   There are large Haitian communities in Miami, New York, and Boston.

_____   10.   The transition from French colonial rule to independence took place peacefully in **Algérie.**

_____   11.   Most of the inhabitants of **Maghreb** are Moslem.

_____   12.   French is spoken in many parts of West and Central Africa as a result of colonization by **la France** and **la Belgique.**

_____   13.   **Léopold Sédar Senghor** is an internationally acclaimed poet and African statesman.

_____   14.   **Le Viêt-nam, le Laos,** and **le Cambodge** formerly made up **l'Indochine.**

_____   15.   **La Francophonie** is primarily an economic movement, created to promote French commerce throughout the world.

Unit Test 2B

A.   Visitons les pays francophones! In Unit 2 we have investigated the Francophone world. You will hear five short descriptions. Listen carefully to the descriptions and then choose the most logical answer. (20 points)

MODEL:

0.   Kerlyne habite probablement ___**d**___.

   (a) en Gaspésie   (b) en Nouvelle Angleterre   (c) en Algérie   (d) en Haïti

1.   Anne habite probablement _____.

   (a) à Zurich   (b) à Montréal   (c) en Nouvelle Calédonie   (d) à Dakar

2.   Lamine étudie probablement _____.

   (a) la médecine   (b) le français   (c) l'informatique   (d) le commerce

3.   Michel habite probablement _____.

   (a) au Québec   (b) en Louisiane   (c) au Luxembourg   (d) en Suisse

4.   Isabelle habite probablement _____.

   (a) au Maghreb   (b) au Sénégal   (c) en Belgique   (d) au Viêt-nam

5.   Hamadi étudie probablement _____.

   (a) la biologie   (b) la danse   (c) l'informatique   (d) l'arabe

B.   Quelle heure est-il? Below are six clock faces, each identified by a letter. As you hear each time stated, select the corresponding clock and write the letter on your answer sheet. First, listen to the model. Then write in the letters as you listen to the speaker. (10 points)

MODEL:

0.   ___**F.**___

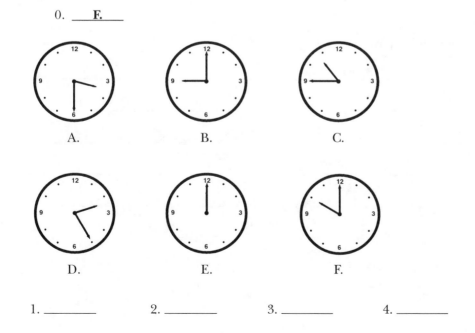

1. _____   2. _____   3. _____   4. _____   5. _____

C. Trois amis. You will hear six statements about the activities of three apartment mates. If all of them are performing the activity, mark the first row: **pluriel.** If only one person is performing the activity, mark the second row: **singulier.** If it is impossible to tell, mark the third row: **impossible à dire.** (12 points)

	0	00	1	2	3	4	5	6
pluriel	✓							
singulier								
impossible à dire		✓						

D. La vie de Christine. You will hear five sentences about Christine, each one containing a number. Listen carefully and write the appropriate numeral in the corresponding blank. (10 points)

MODEL:

0. Elle travaille à _____4_____ heures.

1. Christine dîne à _____ heures.

2. Elle ne regarde pas la télé après _____ heures.

3. Elle habite _____, avenue du Maine.

4. Elle habite l'appartement numéro _____.

5. Elle travaille _____ heures par semaine.

E. La réponse est non! Let's disagree! Listen carefully to each sentence and then write the opposite (the negative form). *Do not* write the affirmative form. (15 points)

MODEL:

0: J'étudie.   You write: **Je n'étudie pas.**

1. _____

2. _____

3. _____

4. _____

5. _____

F. Questions personnelles. Your professor finds you fascinating. Answer the following questions in complete sentences so he/she can get to know you. (18 points)

1. _____

2. _____

3. _____

4. _____

5. _____

6. _____

G. Culture. Read the following statements about Francophone culture. Write (V) for **vrai** if you think the statement is true and (F) for **faux** if you think the statement is false. (15 points)

_____ 1. French claims on the American continent ended in 1763 as a result of the French and Indian war.

_____ 2. One of the first French settlements in Canada was called **l'Acadie.**

_____ 3. In **Québec** the majority of the population is **francophone.**

_____ 4. **Les Séparatistes** in the province of **Québec** want to separate from Canada for economic reasons.

_____ 5. Not many Cajuns speak French anymore.

_____ 6. Cajun culture has been influenced by French, African, and Native American cultures.

_____ 7. **Toussaint-Louverture** and **Jean-Jacques Dessalines** led their people to freedom from slavery and French rule.

_____ 8. **Haïti** was the first self-governed state in North America for people of African ancestry.

_____ 9. The countries of **Algérie, Maroc,** and **Tunisie** are called **le Maghreb.**

_____ 10. As a result of independence, French is no longer spoken in **le Maroc.**

_____ 11. French is the official language in many sub-Saharan African countries.

_____ 12. **La France** does not have good relations with the countries of West and Central Africa.

_____ 13. The political, philosophical, and literary movement known as **la Négritude** depicts the African diaspora in a negative light.

_____ 14. The Senegalese writer **David Diop** sang the praises of French culture in Africa in his work and opposed independence from French rule for **Sénégal.**

_____ 15. Because of **l'Union européenne,** Bruxelles is becoming an important political center in Europe.

Test Sheets: Unit Test 2B   **TP   35**

Unit Test 3A

A. Des amis. You will hear five statements about various people. If the noun in the sentence is masculine, mark row one: **masculin.** If the noun in the sentence is feminine, mark row two: **féminin.** If it is impossible to tell, mark the third row: **impossible à dire.** (10 points)

	0	00	1	2	3	4	5
masculin	√						
féminin		√					
impossible à dire							

B. Logique ou illogique? You will hear five pairs of sentences. For each pair, decide whether the second action logically follows the first action, and mark either **logique** or **illogique** on the chart below. (10 points)

	0	1	2	3	4	5
logique	√					
illogique						

C. Une chambre d'étudiant(e). Answer the following questions affirmatively or negatively according to the picture below. (10 points)

MODEL:

0. **Oui, il y a des livres.**

1. _____

2. _____

3. _____

4. _____

5. _____

D. Demain aussi. Listen to what the following people are doing. Then say that tomorrow they are going to do the same things. (10 points)

MODEL:

0. Demain aussi, **je vais jouer du piano.**

1. Demain aussi, _____.

2. Demain aussi, _____.

3. Demain aussi, _____.

4. Demain aussi, _____.

5. Demain aussi, _____.

E. Questions personnelles. Answer the questions you hear in complete sentences. Write only your answer, not the question. (15 points)

1. _____

2. _____

3. _____

4. _____

5. _____

F. Vous êtes sophistiqué(e)! Make the following sentences more sophisticated by combining each of the pairs of sentences below into *one* sentence. Pay close attention to word order. (18 points)

MODELS:

0. Voici un café. Il est petit. **Voici un petit café.**
00. Voici des amis. Ils sont suisses. **Voici des amis suisses.**

1. Voici une copine. Elle est brillante. _____

2. Voici des professeurs. Ils sont patients. _____

3. Voici un ordinateur. Il est bon. _____

4. Voici des voitures. Elles sont jolies. _____

5. Voici un café. Il est mauvais. _____

G. Lettre à un copain. Jean-Michel thinks his cousin Christine and his friend Olivier might like each other. In the following letter he describes Christine. Complete his letter with the appropriate words from the word bank below. You will not use them all, but you may use some more than once. (14 points)

au, à la, c'est, de, de la, elle est, la, le, l', un, une, du

Cher Olivier,

Ma cousine s'appelle Christine. Comment est-elle? _____ très intelligente, mais

_____ une fille très timide. Elle joue _____ piano, mais elle ne joue

pas très bien. Elle adore _____ art et elle va souvent _____ musée

avec moi. _____ très sophistiquée. Elle a beaucoup d'amis, mais _____

une personne égoïste. Voici son adresse: 10bis, rue Daguerre, 75014 Paris. Si tu préfères le courrier

électronique, son adresse internet est christi2004@aol.fr.

Amitiés,

Jean-Michel

H. Vous avez une opinion? Reread Jean-Michel's letter to Olivier. After making a list of her good and bad qualities, decide if Olivier will like Christine or not, by checking off the appropriate box below. (5 points: 2 points per category + 1 for checking box)

Bonnes qualités   *Mauvaises qualités*

Elle est _____   Elle est _____

_____   _____

_____   _____

☐ Olivier va aimer Christine.   ☐ Olivier ne va pas aimer Christine.

I.   Une question de culture. In the **Notes culturelles** of Lessons 7, 8, and 9 you learned about some of the differences between French and American culture. Read the sentences below and mark "V" for **vrai** if you think the statement is true and "F" for **faux,** if you think the statement is false. (8 points)

_____ 1. **Un VTT** can be used on hilly terrain as well as in the city.

_____ 2. **Les deux-roues** such as the **mobylette** are used mostly by older persons.

_____ 3. The French call people-watching in cafés **le septième art.**

_____ 4. **La Cité Universitaire** for university students in Paris is located in **le Quartier latin.**

_____ 5. **Les cafés** are as much a social institution as they are a place to have **un express.**

_____ 6. **La Palme d'or** is the top award at **le Festival de Cannes.**

_____ 7. The French government is virtually unwilling to support French **cinéma.**

_____ 8. **Un pourboire** is ordinarily given to the person who sells you a ticket at the box office.

Unit Test 3B

A.   Des amis. You will hear five statements about various people. If the noun in the sentence is masculine, mark row one: **masculin.** If the noun in the sentence is feminine, mark row two: **féminin.** If it is impossible to tell, mark the third row: **impossible à dire.** (10 points)

	0	00	1	2	3	4	5
masculin		√					
féminin	√						
impossible à dire							

B.   Logique ou illogique? You will hear five pairs of sentences. For each pair, decide whether the second action logically follows the first action, and mark either **logique** or **illogique** on the chart below. (10 points)

	0	1	2	3	4	5
logique	√					
illogique						

C. Une chambre d'étudiant(e). Answer the following questions affirmatively or negatively according to the picture below. (10 points)

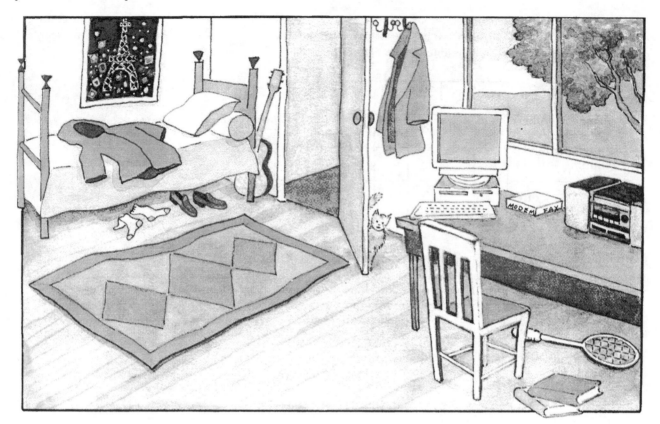

MODEL:

    0. Oui, il y a des livres.

    1. _____

    2. _____

    3. _____

    4. _____

    5. _____

D. Demain aussi. Listen to what the following people are doing. Then say that tomorrow they are going to do the same things. (10 points)

MODEL:

    0. Demain aussi, **je vais travailler.**

    1. Demain aussi, _____.

    2. Demain aussi, _____.

    3. Demain aussi, _____.

    4. Demain aussi, _____.

    5. Demain aussi, _____.

E. Questions personnelles. Answer the questions you hear in complete sentences. Write only your answer, not the question. (15 points)

1. _____

2. _____

3. _____

4. _____

5. _____

F. Vous êtes sophistiqué(e)! Make the following sentences more sophisticated by combining each of the pairs of sentences below into *one* sentence. Pay close attention to word order. (18 points)

MODELS:

   0. Voici un café. Il est petit.   **Voici un petit café.**
 00. Voici des amis. Ils sont suisses.   **Voici des amis suisses.**

1. Voici une femme. Elle est mariée. _____

2. Voici une fille. Elle est heureuse. _____

3. Voici une piscine. Elle est grande. _____

4. Voici un garçon. Il est timide. _____

5. Voici des étudiants. Ils sont américains. _____

6. Voici des montres. Elles sont jolies. _____

G. Lettre à une amie. Christine thinks her cousin Jean-Michel and her friend Jeannette would make a great couple. In the following letter she describes Jean-Michel. Complete her letter with the appropriate words from the word bank below. You will not use them all and you may use some more than once. (14 points: 2 points each)

au, à la, c'est, de, de la, il est, le, la, l', un

Chère Jeannette,

    Mon cousin s'appelle Jean-Michel. Comment est-il? _____ un garçon très

dynamique. En général, _____ très amusant, mais _____ un garçon

pénible quand il n'est pas content. Il joue très bien _____ guitare. Il adore

_____ sport et il joue souvent _____ volley avec moi. Si je joue bien,

_____ très désagréable. Voici son adresse: 49, rue du Four, 75006 Paris. Si tu préfères le

courrier électronique, voici son adresse Internet: JM2003@aol.fr.

Amitiés,

Christine

        Test Sheets: Unit Test 3B **TP** **43**

H. Vous avez une opinion? Re-read Christine's letter to Jeannette. After making a list of his good and bad qualities, decide if Jeannette will like Jean-Michel or not, by checking off the appropriate box below. (5 points: 2 points per category + 1 for checking box)

Bonnes qualités

Il est _____

_____

_____

☐ Jeannette va aimer Jean-Michel.

Mauvaises qualités

Il est _____

_____

_____

☐ Jeannette ne va pas aimer Jean-Michel.

I. Une question de culture. In the **Notes culturelles** of Lessons 7, 8, and 9 you learned about some of the differences between French and American culture. Read the sentences below and mark "V" for **vrai** if you think the statement is true and "F" for **faux** if you think the statement is false. (8 points)

_____ 1. It is unusual for young people to have **un VTT** in France.

_____ 2. **Les deux-roues** are very safe and extremely popular in **l'Hexagone.**

_____ 3. **Une cité universitaire** is just like an American college campus.

_____ 4. **La terrasse** is usually located outside **un café.**

_____ 5. At **un café,** one can eat or drink, people-watch, chat with friends, relax, or study.

_____ 6. *Le Nouvel Observateur* is a daily newspaper.

_____ 7. **Le cinéma** is considered a serious art form in France.

_____ 8. **Le Festival de Cannes** showcases American blockbusters and not much else.

Unit Test 4A

A. Le budget de Dominique. You will hear about Dominique's budget. Fill in the amounts of her expenses or income for each item. (15 points: 3 points each)

loyer: _____   bourse: _____

transports: _____   téléphone: _____   loisirs: _____

B. Dans la maison. You will hear four sentences describing what the six members of the Boudin family are doing. Then indicate which room they are probably in by choosing the appropriate letter. (8 points)

MODEL:

0. Médor est dans ___**a**___ .

   (a) le jardin   (b) la salle à manger   (c) le salon

1. Michel et Marc Boudin sont dans _____.

   (a) la salle à manger   (b) la cuisine   (c) la salle de bains

2. Grand-mère Boudin est dans _____.

   (a) le salon   (b) les W.C.   (c) le jardin

3. Monsieur et Madame Boudin sont dans _____.

   (a) le garage   (b) la chambre   (c) la salle à manger

4. Marie Boudin est dans _____.

   (a) sa chambre   (b) la salle de séjour   (c) la cuisine

C. Une question de culture. You will hear five statements about French culture. Listen carefully and decide whether each statement is true (**vrai**) or false (**faux**). (10 points)

	0	1	2	3	4	5
vrai	✓					
faux						

D. Possessions. We all like to brag. Listen carefully to the following people bragging about their possessions and then complete the sentences below with the appropriate possessive adjectives. (12 points)

MODELS:

0. C'est ___**mon**___ appartement.

00. Ce sont ___**tes**___ meubles.

1. C'est _____ maison.   4. C'est _____ tailleur.

2. Ce sont _____ chaussures.   5. C'est _____ cravate.

3. C'est _____ studio.   6. C'est _____ jean.

E. Activités. Listen to the things these procrastinators plan on doing in the future. Imagine that they decide to do these things right away and express what they're doing in the present tense, according to the model. (15 points)

MODEL:

   0. **Je cherche un appartement.**

   1. _____

   2. _____

   3. _____

   4. _____

   5. _____

F. Comparaisons personnelles. Listen to each question carefully and then express your opinion with a complete sentence. (12 points)

   1. _____

   2. _____

   3. _____

G. Vêtements. Describe what your instructor is wearing today. Write at least four complete sentences. Don't forget to include colors. (16 points: 4 points per sentence)

_____

_____

_____

_____

_____

H. Une chambre d'étudiant(e). Here's a description of a typical dorm room. Choose the most logical word to complete each sentence. (12 points)

   1. L'ordinateur est _____ bureau.

      (a) sous le   (b) sur le   (c) devant le

   2. Le lit est _____ fenêtre.

      (a) près de la   (b) derrière la   (c) dans la

   3. La chaise est _____ bureau.

      (a) sur le   (b) devant le   (c) loin du

   4. Des livres, des chaussures et d'autres objets sont _____ lit.

      (a) par le   (b) entre le   (c) sous le

Unit Test 4B

A. Le budget d'Isabelle. You will hear about Isabelle's budget. Fill in the amounts of her expenses or income for each item. (15 points: 3 points each)

loyer: _____ salaire: _____

vêtements: _____ Internet: _____ repas: _____

B. Dans la maison. You will hear four sentences describing what five members of the Boudin family are doing. Then indicate which room they are probably in by choosing the appropriate letter. (8 points)

MODEL:

   0. Médor est dans ___**a**___ .

     (a) le jardin   (b) la salle à manger   (c) le salon

   1. Monsieur Boudin est dans _____.

     (a) le salon   (b) la cuisine   (c) les WC

   2. Madame Boudin est dans _____.

     (a) la salle de bains   (b) le garage   (c) la salle à manger

   3. Michel Boudin est dans _____.

     (a) le jardin   (b) la salle de séjour   (c) sa chambre

   4. Marie et Marc Boudin sont dans _____.

     (a) la salle de séjour   (b) les toilettes   (c) le jardin

C. Une question de culture. You will hear five statements about French culture. Listen carefully and decide whether each statement is true (**vrai**) or false (**faux**). (10 points)

	0	1	2	3	4	5
vrai	✓					
faux						

D. Possessions. We all like to brag. Listen carefully to the following people bragging about their possessions and then complete the sentences below with the appropriate possessive adjectives. (12 points)

MODELS:

   0. C'est ___**mon**___ appartement.

  00. Ce sont ___**tes**___ meubles.

   1. C'est _____ chambre.   4. C'est _____ pantalon.

   2. C'est _____ jardin.   5. C'est _____ pull.

   3. Ce sont _____ lunettes de soleil.

E. Activités. Listen to the things these procrastinators plan on doing in the future. Imagine that they decide to do these things right away and express what they're doing in the present tense, according to the model. (15 points)

MODEL:

    0. **Je cherche un appartement.**

    1. _____

    2. _____

    3. _____

    4. _____

    5. _____

F. Comparaisons personnelles. Listen to each question carefully and then express your opinion with a complete sentence. (12 points).

    1. _____

    2. _____

    3. _____

G. Vêtements. Write a paragraph describing what your instructor is wearing today. Write at least four complete sentences. Don't forget to include colors. (16 points: 4 points per sentence)

_____

_____

_____

_____

H. Une chambre d'étudiant(e). Write four sentences describing your room using one element from each column in every sentence (you will not necessarily use all the vocabulary given). (12 points)

L'ordinateur	est	près de	la porte
Le lit	sont	sur	la fenêtre
Les chaussettes		dans	le bureau
La table		sous	le lit
Le téléphone		à côté de	l'ordinateur
Les chaussures		devant	la chaise
Les livres			la lampe

    1. _____

    2. _____

    3. _____

    4. _____

Unit Test 5A

A. Dates historiques. You will hear five statements about important events in French history. Write the dates in the blanks. (10 points)

MODEL:

    0. Guillaume le Conquérant a gagné la Bataille de Hastings en ____**1066**____.

    1. Jeanne d'Arc a délivré Orléans en _____.

    2. En _____, Napoléon est devenu empereur.

    3. En _____, Marie Antoinette a été guillotinée.

    4. Philippe-Auguste est mort en _____.

    5. Henri IV a été assassiné en _____.

B. Voyage au présent ou voyage au passé? You will hear six statements. Some refer to a trip that is currently taking place. Others refer to a trip that took place sometime last year. Listen carefully to the verb. If the verb is in the present tense, mark row one: **présent.** If the verb is in the passé composé, mark row two: **passé composé.** (6 points)

	0	00	1	2	3	4	5	6
présent	✓							
passé composé		✓						

C. Combien? You will hear five statements about various people. If the subject of the sentence is singular, mark row one: **singulier.** If the subject of the sentence is plural, mark row two: **pluriel.** (5 points)

	0	00	1	2	3	4	5
singulier	✓						
pluriel		✓					

D. Une question de culture. You will hear five statements about different aspects of French culture. Indicate whether they are true **(vrai)** or false **(faux).** (10 points)

	0	1	2	3	4	5
vrai	✓					
faux						

E. Hier aussi. Listen to what is happening and/or what the following people are doing. Then say that yesterday the same things happened. Use the **passé composé.** (21 points)

MODEL:

    0. Hier aussi, **il a joué au tennis.**

    1. Hier aussi, elle _____.

    2. Hier aussi, nous _____.

    3. Hier aussi, il _____.

    4. Hier aussi, vous _____.

    5. Hier aussi, tu _____.

    6. Hier aussi, ils _____.

    7. Hier aussi, je (j') _____.

F. Conseils. You are babysitting your three-year-old cousin. She is feeling sad and missing her parents. Choose the best response to each request she makes. (16 points)

    1. J'ai peur des monstres! _____

        (a) Regardons un film d'horreur!   (b) Allons dans la cuisine!   (c) N'aie pas peur!

    2. J'ai envie de parler à ma maman. _____

        (a) Téléphonons à ta mère!   (b) Ne sois pas pénible!   (c) J'ai sommeil.

    3. J'ai perdu mon nounours (*teddy bear*). _____

        (a) Va au lit!   (b) Loue un vélo!   (c) Cherchons ton nounours!

    4. Je veux mon papa. _____

        (a) Attends un peu! Il arrive.   (b) Fais tes devoirs!   (c) Jouons au tennis!

G. Message. Two French students have invited you to a concert next week. You are not feeling well (you have mononucleosis) and are very tired. If you fill in the following letter with the expressions in the word bank, you can thank them for the invitation. You may need to make the sentence negative. (12 points)

avoir 18 ans   avoir besoin   avoir chaud   avoir envie
avoir faim   avoir froid   avoir l'intention   avoir peur
avoir raison   avoir soif   avoir sommeil   avoir tort

Chers amis,

    C'est très gentil de m'inviter, mais je ne peux pas aller au concert. Je suis très malade. Le

docteur dit que j'ai la mononucléose. Je (J') _____ de sortir.

Je (J') _____ tout le temps; je dors 12 heures par jour! En plus,

je ne mange pas, je (j') _____. Pourtant *(however)*, je

bois trois litres d'eau par jour, je (j') _____ tout le temps! Le médecin

dit que je dois rester au lit pendant un mois. J'espère qu'il _____!

Je (J') _____ de voir mes amis!

     Je vous embrasse. (XOXO)

_____ *(Votre signature)*

H. Le week-end dernier. Write a short paragraph of five sentences about what you did last weekend. Be creative! Use the **passé composé.** (20 points: 15 points for accuracy of communication, 5 points for imagination and vocabulary)

_____

_____

_____

_____

_____

            Test Sheets: Unit Test 5A **TP 51**

Unit Test 5B

A. Dates historiques. You will hear five statements about important events in French history. Write the dates in the blanks. (10 points)

Model:

0. François 1er est né en ____**1494**____.

1. Guillaume la Conquérant a gagné la Bataille de Hastings en _____.

2. En _____, Jeanne d'Arc est morte brûlée vive *(burned alive)*.

3. Le 14 juillet _____, la Révolution française a commencé.

4. La Deuxième Guerre mondiale a fini en _____.

5. En janvier de l'an _____, l'Europe va adopter l'euro.

B. Voyage au présent ou voyage au passé? You will hear six statements. Some refer to a trip that is currently taking place. Others refer to a trip that took place sometime last year. Listen carefully to the verb. If the verb is in the present tense, mark row one: **présent**. If the verb is in the passé composé, mark row two: **passé composé.** (6 points)

	0	00	1	2	3	4	5	6
présent	✓							
passé composé		✓						

C. Combien? You will hear five statements about various people. If the subject of the sentence is singular, mark row one: **singulier.** If the subject of the sentence is plural, mark row two: **pluriel.** (5 points)

	0	00	1	2	3	4	5
singulier	✓						
pluriel		✓					

D. Une question de culture. You will hear five statements about different aspects of French culture. Indicate whether they are true (**vrai**) or false (**faux**). (10 points)

	0	1	2	3	4	5
vrai	✓					
faux						

E. Hier aussi. Listen to what is happening and/or what the following people are doing. Then say that yesterday the same things happened. Use the **passé composé.** (21 points)

MODEL:

0. Hier aussi, **elle a visité Rome.**

1. Hier aussi, elle _____ .

2. Hier aussi, ils _____ .

3. Hier aussi, il _____ .

4. Hier aussi, vous _____ .

5. Hier aussi, ils _____ .

6. Hier aussi, je (j') _____ .

7. Hier aussi, nous _____ .

F. Conseils. Your French classmate has to take an important exam and he needs your expert advice. Choose the best advice in each case from the choices below. (16 points)

1. Je n'ai pas été sérieux ce semestre. _____
    (a) Sois sérieux aujourd'hui!
    (b) Va au cinéma cet après-midi!
    (c) Rends visite aux copains!

2. Je n'ai pas étudié cette semaine. _____
    (a) Étudie la semaine prochaine!
    (b) Commence à étudier aujourd'hui!
    (c) Écoute un CD de M. C. Solaar!

3. Je ne suis pas allé en classe la semaine dernière. _____
    (a) Va en classe cette semaine!
    (b) Invite une amie au musée!
    (c) Reste chez toi!

4. Je n'ai pas réussi au dernier examen. _____
    (a) Organise une fête!
    (b) Achète un cadeau pour le professeur!
    (c) N'aie pas peur!

G. Message. You are in love with a French exchange student and he/she is returning to France tomorrow. Complete the following letter with expressions from the word bank so he/she knows how you feel. You may need to make certain sentences negative. (12 points)

avoir 18 ans	avoir besoin	avoir chaud	avoir envie
avoir faim	avoir froid	avoir l'intention	avoir peur
avoir raison	avoir soif	avoir sommeil	avoir tort

Cher Jean-Pierre (Chère Marie-France),

Je sais que je suis très jeune; j'_____ et tu as 22 ans, mais

j'_____ de te parler de mes sentiments. Tu es un garçon (une fille)

formidable et je crois que tu me trouves bien aussi. Est-ce que j'_____?

Maintenant, tu rentres en France et j'_____ que tu trouves un(e)

autre petit(e) ami(e)! Est-ce que tu _____ de m'envoyer du courrier

électronique de France? J'espère que oui. J'_____ de rester en

contact avec toi.

Ton ami(e) qui t'aime,

_____ (*Votre signature*)

H. Le week-end dernier. Write a short paragraph of five sentences about what you did last weekend. Use the **passé composé**. (20 points: 15 points for accuracy of communication, 5 points for imagination and vocabulary)

_____

_____

_____

_____

_____

Aperçu culturel
La France et ses régions (Version 5A)

A. Quatre régions françaises. Match the following descriptions with the regions they describe by writing the appropriate word after each description. (20 points)

l'Alsace   la Normandie   Île-de-France   la Provence

1. Les premières troupes alliées ont débarqué dans cette région pendant la Deuxième Guerre

    mondiale. _____

2. Cette région est connue pour ses monuments et ses musées. _____

3. Cette région a inspiré Van Gogh, Matisse, Cézanne et Picasso. _____

4. L'architecture, les traditions et la cuisine de cette région sont très influencées par

    l'Allemagne. _____

B. L'histoire et les régions. Choose the answer that best completes each sentence below. (40 points)

1. L'architecte I. M. Pei a construit _____ au vingtième siècle.

    (a) la Tour Eiffel   (b) la Pyramide du Louvre   (c) les Champs-Élysées

2. La Normandie est devenue indépendante sous _____ en 911.

    (a) les Vikings   (b) les Celtes   (c) les Français

3. _____ a commandé les armées alliées en Normandie pendant *(during)* la Deuxième

    Guerre mondiale.

    (a) Le Président Roosevelt   (b) Winston Churchill   (c) Le Général Eisenhower

4. Gustave Eiffel a construit la Tour Eiffel en _____.

    (a) l'an 2000   (b) 1945   (c) 1889

5. La tribu _____ des Parisii a fondé Paris en 350 av. J-C.

    (a) française   (b) allemande   (c) celte

6. _____ a été la résidence des papes au quatorzième siècle.

    (a) Avignon   (b) Paris   (c) Strasbourg

7. Le Duc de Normandie est devenu roi _____ en 1066.

    (a) d'Angleterre   (b) d'Espagne   (c) de France

8. _____ est un musée qui a longtemps été une résidence royale à Paris.

    (a) Le Musée d'Orsay   (b) Le Louvre   (c) Versailles

C. Un voyage imaginaire. Your instructor gets a grant which allows him/her to send one lucky student on a trip to one of the regions in France described in *La France et ses régions.* You know you would benefit from such an experience. Explain where you would like to go and what you would see and do there. (40 points: 30 points for linguistic accuracy, 10 points for imagination and vocabulary)

_____

_____

_____

_____

_____

_____

_____

_____

_____

Aperçu culturel
La France et ses régions (Version 5B)

A. Quatre régions françaises. Match the following descriptions with the regions they describe by writing the appropriate word after each description. (20 points)

l'Alsace   la Normandie   Île-de-France   la Provence

1. Le parlement de l'Union européenne a été établi dans la plus grande ville de cette région.

   _____

2. Cette région est le centre du pays et de beaucoup de ses activités. _____

3. Beaucoup de soldats américains ont vu les plages de cette région pour la première fois pendant la

   Deuxième Guerre mondiale. _____

4. Les touristes apprécient ses beaux paysages et son climat très doux. _____

B. L'histoire et les régions. Choose the answer that best completes each sentence below. (40 points)

1. On trouve la *Joconde (Mona Lisa)* _____.
   (a) aux Champs-Élysées   (b) au Musée d'Orsay   (c) au Louvre

2. _____, un duc français, a été couronné roi d'Angleterre en 1066.
   (a) Guillaume le Conquérant   (b) Édouard d'Angleterre   (c) Henri IV

3. _____ est une abbaye située en Normandie. On a commencé sa construction en 1023.
   (a) Notre Dame   (b) Le Mont-Saint-Michel   (c) Le Boulevard Saint-Michel

4. En Alsace, il y a eu de nombreux conflits entre _____ et la France.
   (a) l'Allemagne   (b) l'Angleterre   (c) la Suisse

5. _____ a été décorée de 20.000 lumières pour marquer l'entrée de la France dans le nouveau

   millénaire dans l'an 2000.
   (a) La pyramide du Louvre   (b) La Tour Eiffel   (c) La Sorbonne

6. La Sorbonne, l'université la plus ancienne de France, a été fondée à Paris _____.
   (a) au douzième siècle   (b) au treizième siècle   (c) au seizième siècle

7. Pour voir les tableaux impressionnistes de Manet, Degas, Monet, Van Gogh et Cézanne, on doit

   aller _____.
   (a) au Louvre   (b) au Musée d'Orsay   (c) à l'Arc de Triomphe

8. Au quatorzième siècle, _____ est le centre religieux et artistique de l'Europe.
   (a) Avignon   (b) Nice   (c) Paris

     Test Sheets: Aperçu culturel **TP 59**

C. Un voyage imaginaire. You have just been on a trip to France. Imagine that you are showing people photos from your vacation. Explain to them what they are seeing, and where the shot was taken. Feel free to express your opinion on the different places you visited. (30 points: 20 points for linguistic accuracy, 10 points for imagination and vocabulary)

_____

_____

_____

_____

_____

_____

_____

_____

_____

Unit Test 6A

A. Combien? You will hear five statements about various people. If the subject of the sentence is singular, mark row one: **singulier.** If the subject of the sentence is plural, mark row two: **pluriel.** (10 points)

	0	00	1	2	3	4	5
singulier	✓						
pluriel		✓					

B. Présent ou passé? You will hear five statements. Listen carefully. If the verb is in the present tense, mark row one: **présent.** If the verb is in the passé composé, mark row two: **passé composé.** (10 points)

	0	00	1	2	3	4	5
présent	✓						
passé composé		✓					

C. Vrai ou faux? You will hear six statements. Indicate whether each one is true (**vrai**) or false (**faux**). (12 points)

	0	1	2	3	4	5	6
vrai							
faux	✓						

D. Questions personnelles. Answer the questions you hear with complete sentences. Write only your answer (not the question). (12 points)

1. _____

2. _____

3. _____

4. _____

E. Un repas d'anniversaire. Complete the following description of your ideal birthday dinner. Don't forget to use the partitive! (12 points: 2 points per item)

1. Comme hors d'œuvre, il y a _____

2. Comme viande ou poisson, il y a _____

3. Comme légumes, il y a _____

4. Comme dessert, il y a _____

5. Comme boissons, il y a _____ et _____

F.   Le champagne. Fill in the blanks as appropriate. (16 points)

1.   Il n'y a pas _____ champagne à la carte.

2.   Aimez-vous _____ champagne?

3.   Combien _____ champagne voulez-vous?

4.   Philippe a bu beaucoup trop _____ champagne hier soir.

5.   J'ai un cousin qui adore _____ champagne français.

6.   Prenez-vous _____ champagne avec vos repas?

7.   _____ champagne va bien avec le poisson.

8.   Il y a _____ champagne au réfrigérateur.

G.   Où ça? Choose the correct preposition to complete the sentences below about Gaël, who loves to travel.
(12 points)

1.   J'ai fait mon premier voyage _____ États-Unis à l'âge de 10 ans. Avec mes parents, bien sûr!
     (a) à la   (b) aux   (c) des

2.   On est allés partout: _____ Californie, _____ Texas et _____ Boston!
     (a) en, au, à   (b) de la, du, en   (c) en, au, en

3.   À 15 ans, j'ai fait un échange _____ Japon. C'est un pays formidable!
     (a) en   (b) au   (c) à

4.   À 17 ans, mon oncle m'a amenée _____ Sénégal. J'adore _____ Afrique.
     (a) au, l'   (b) en, en   (c) à, l'

5.   Ma petite amie, Chloé, vient _____ Suisse. J'ai très envie de visiter _____ Suisse, un jour.
     (a) de la, la   (b) à, la   (c) de, la

6.   Mon meilleur ami vient _____ Brésil. Donc, l'année prochaine je vais visiter _____ Brésil!
     (a) de, au   (b) de la, au   (c) du, le

H.   Composition: Joséphine est en excellente forme. Joséphine is in terrific shape. How does she manage?
Use four different verbs and your imagination! (16 points: 4 points per sentence)

Write two sentences describing things she does.

_____

_____

Write two sentences describing things she does not do.

_____

_____

Unit Test 6B

A. Combien? You will hear five statements about various people. If the subject of the sentence is singular, mark row one: **singulier.** If the subject of the sentence is plural, mark row two: **pluriel.** (10 points)

	0	00	1	2	3	4	5
singulier	✓						
pluriel		✓					

B. Présent ou passé? You will hear five statements. Listen carefully. If the verb is in the present tense, mark row one: **présent.** If the verb is in the passé composé, mark row two: **passé composé.** (10 points)

	0	00	1	2	3	4	5
présent	✓						
passé composé		✓					

C. Vrai ou faux? You will hear six statements. Indicate whether each one is true **(vrai)** or false **(faux).** (12 points)

	0	1	2	3	4	5	6
vrai	✓						
faux							

D. Questions personnelles. Answer the questions you hear with complete sentences. Write only your answer (not the question). (12 points)

1. _____

2. _____

3. _____

4. _____

E. Un repas romantique. Complete the following description of a romantic dinner you are preparing for your boyfriend or girlfriend. Don't forget to use the partitive! (12 points: 2 points per item)

1. Comme hors d'œuvre, il y a _____

2. Comme viande ou poisson, il y a _____

3. Comme légumes, il y a _____

4. Comme dessert, il y a _____

5. Comme boissons, il y a _____ et _____

F. Le Coca. Fill in the blanks as appropriate. (16 points)

1. Je déteste _____ Coca.

2. Il y a trop _____ sucre dans le Coca.

3. Achète _____ Coca pour la fête, s'il te plaît.

4. Je prends toujours _____ Coca avec le déjeuner.

5. Magali ne prend pas _____ Coca; elle est au régime.

6. Aimez-vous _____ Coca ou préférez-vous _____ Coca light?

7. J'ai commandé _____ Coca parce que j'ai soif.

8. On pense que les Américains boivent beaucoup _____ Coca.

G. Où ça? Choose the correct preposition to complete the sentences below about Cunégonde, who loves to travel. (12 points)

1. Je suis venue _____ États-Unis pour vivre _____ France à l'âge de 10 ans. Avec mes parents, bien sûr!

   (a) à la, la   (b) aux, à   (c) des, en

2. On a beaucoup voyagé: _____ Normandie, _____ Alpes et _____ Nice!

   (a) en, dans les, à   (b) de la, des, à   (c) en, au, à

3. À 15 ans, j'ai fait un échange _____ Irlande. Les Irlandais sont très gentils!

   (a) en   (b) au   (c) à

4. À 17 ans, ma grand-mère m'a amenée _____ Portugal où nous avons de la famille.

   (a) en   (b) au   (c) aux

5. Ma meilleure amie, Simona, vient _____ Italie. J'ai rendu visite à ma copine et à sa famille l'année dernière.

   (a) de la   (b) de   (c) d'

6. Plus tard, je veux aller vivre _____ Chine pour apprendre le chinois! Bonne idée, non?

   (a) en   (b) à   (c) le

H. Yannick est trop maigre (*skinny*)! Yannick thinks that he's too thin; he would like to look like Jean-Claude Van Damme. He has hired a personal trainer to help him "bulk up." You are his personal trainer. What is Yannick doing to increase his muscle mass and gain weight? Write four sentences describing things he is doing. Use four different verbs and your imagination! (12 points: 3 points per sentence)

_____

_____

_____

_____

Unit Test 7A

A. Logique ou illogique? Listen to the five pairs of sentences and decide whether they are logical (**logique**) or illogical (**illogique**). (10 points)

	0	1	2	3	4	5
logique	✓					
illogique						

B. Les étudiants universitaires. You are going to hear eight sentences about some students at an American university. If the subject of the sentence is singular, mark **singulier.** If the subject of the sentence is plural, mark **pluriel.** If it is impossible to say one way or another, mark **singulier ou pluriel.** (16 points)

	0	00	000	1	2	3	4	5	6	7	8
singulier	✓										
pluriel		✓									
singulier ou pluriel			✓								

C. L'éducation en France. Listen to the following sentences on education in France and indicate whether they are **vrai** (true) or **faux** (false). (12 points)

	0	1	2	3	4	5	6
vrai	✓						
faux							

D. Questions: la vie à l'université. Answer the following questions. Use object pronouns in your answers. (15 points)

MODEL:

   0. **Oui, je les aime.**

   1. _____

   2. _____

   3. _____

   4. _____

   5. _____

   6. _____

E. Mais non! You're having one of those days. Answer every question in the negative. Replace the underlined words with object pronouns. Watch out, the last one is in the command form! (10 points)

1. Vous cherchez <u>le prof</u>? Non, je _____.

2. Vous écoutez <u>mes conseils</u>? Non, je _____.

3. Vous allez écrire <u>à Marie</u>? Non, je _____.

4. Vous avez parlé à <u>vos parents</u>? Non, je _____.

5. Invitons <u>ta cousine</u> ce soir. Non, _____.

F. Vous êtes fascinant(e)! Your professor would like to learn more about you. Answer the following questions about you in complete sentences. (12 points)

1. Quel diplôme préparez-vous? _____

2. Combien de cours suivez-vous? _____

3. Quelle est votre bande dessinée préférée? _____

4. Avez-vous lu un roman récemment? (Si oui, quel roman?) _____

_____

G. Des conseils. You are a career counselor. Choose the best answer to advise the following people who are currently **au chômage** *(out of work)*. (10 points)

1. Mathilde Jacquet a un doctorat en littérature. Elle peut _____.
   (a) être ingénieur
   (b) enseigner la littérature
   (c) travailler dans un laboratoire
   (d) voyager

2. François Galvani prépare un diplôme en chimie. Il peut _____.
   (a) enseigner la littérature
   (b) rater un examen
   (c) faire des recherches
   (d) travailler en gestion

3. Dominique Zami veut devenir docteur. Il doit _____.
   (a) étudier la médecine
   (b) étudier le droit
   (c) étudier le français
   (d) réussir

4. Élisabeth Breton veut faire des études commerciales. Elle doit préparer un diplôme _____.
   (a) en philosophie
   (b) en psychologie
   (c) en électronique
   (d) en publicité

5. Julie Anglésy a obtenu une licence en informatique. Elle peut _____.
   (a) travailler chez IBM
   (b) célébrer
   (c) faire de la sculpture
   (d) enseigner l'histoire de l'art

H. Isidore Intello. Write a short paragraph about a French student named Isidore Intello who is spending the year in the U.S. at your university. He is very motivated and very intelligent. Indicate what kind of courses he is taking. Are all of his courses difficult? What kinds of books does he read in his free time? (Remember, he is a serious guy.) Write about what he does on the weekend. And finally, indicate how his fellow students feel about him. (15 points)

Test Sheets: Unit Test 7A   **TP**

C. Allons en France! You are a journalist for the *New York Times* and because you are fluent in French, you have the opportunity to interview one of the following people: Gérard Depardieu, Catherine Deneuve, Mary Pierce, Zinédine Zidane, or Ousmane Sembene.

Who would you interview? _____

Now write five questions that you would like to ask the celebrity you have chosen. (40 points)

1. _____

_____

2. _____

_____

3. _____

_____

4. _____

_____

5. _____

_____

Aperçu culturel
Culture et loisirs (Version 7B)

A. Vrai ou faux? Read the following statements regarding the **Aperçu culturel** and decide whether they are true (**V**) or false (**F**). (35 points)

_____ 1. La France n'a jamais gagné la Coupe du Monde.

_____ 2. Zinédine Zidane a joué un rôle très important dans la Coupe du Monde que l'équipe de France a remportée *(won)* en 1998.

_____ 3. La Fête de la musique est simplement une excuse pour ne pas aller au travail.

_____ 4. Le cinéma est né en France il y a plus de 200 ans.

_____ 5. Ionesco et Beckett font partie du théâtre de l'Absurde.

_____ 6. Le cinéma africain refuse de traiter certains sujets comme la colonisation.

_____ 7. Les films de la «Nouvelle Vague» ont été réalisés dans les années 60 et 70.

B. Qu'en savez-vous? Choose the best answer to complete each of the following sentences. (35 points)

1. Le cyclisme, le football et le tennis sont _____.
   (a) les sports les moins chers en France
   (b) les sports les plus populaires en France
   (c) peu pratiqués en France

2. Greg Lemond et Lance Armstrong sont _____.
   (a) deux Américains qui ont gagné le Tour de France
   (b) deux Américains qui ont joué dans la Coupe du Monde
   (c) deux Américains qui ont joué à Roland-Garros

3. La Coupe du Monde est traditionnellement dominée par _____.
   (a) le Brésil et l'Argentine
   (b) la France et la Belgique
   (c) les États-Unis

4. En France, le cinéma dépend du soutien _____.
   (a) des adolescents
   (b) de l'État français
   (c) du public français

5. On a commencé à s'intéresser au théâtre en France _____.
   (a) au treizième siècle
   (b) au seizième siècle
   (c) au vingtième siècle

6. Louis et Auguste Lumière ont inventé _____.
   (a) le théâtre
   (b) le Tour de France
   (c) le cinéma

7. En France, au moins 40 pour cent des chansons qu'on entend à la radio doivent être _____.
   (a) francophones
   (b) anglophones
   (c) étrangères

Test Sheets: Aperçu culturel **TP 75**

C. À vous de jouer! You are working for your college newspaper and because of your vast knowledge of French culture you have been chosen to interview Lance Armstrong or Zinédine Zidane for an article.

Who would you choose? _____

Now write five questions you would like to ask that person. (30 points)

1. _____

_____

2. _____

_____

3. _____

_____

4. _____

_____

5. _____

_____

Unit Test 8A

A. Passé composé ou imparfait? You will hear five sentences. Listen to them carefully and then decide if each sentence is in the **passé composé** or the **imparfait.** (10 points)

	0	00	1	2	3	4	5
passé composé	✓						
imparfait		✓					

B. La vie en France. Listen to the following sentences on French culture. Listen carefully and then decide if each sentence is **vrai** (true) or **faux** (false). (12 points)

	0	1	2	3	4	5	6
vrai							
faux	✓						

C. Autrefois. Everyone likes to remember the "good old days." Answer the following questions about your childhood in complete sentences. (12 points)

1. _____

2. _____

3. _____

4. _____

D. Qui? Quoi? Comment? It's not who you know, it's what you know that counts. Complete each question below with either **Sais-tu** or **Connais-tu.** (8 points)

1. _____ si le centre commercial est ouvert le soir?

2. _____ à quelle heure la classe commence?

3. _____ tout le monde dans cette classe?

4. _____ la Martinique et la Guadeloupe?

E. Un événement étrange. Something strange happened to a friend of yours last weekend. To find out what took place complete each sentence with either **qui, que,** or **qu'.** (8 points)

1. Samedi dernier, il y a eu un événement _____ je ne vais pas oublier.

2. Je déjeunais avec une amie _____ était dans la même classe que moi au lycée.

3. Elle m'a montré un joli bracelet _____ on lui avait donné pour son anniversaire.

4. Tout de suite j'ai remarqué _____ c'était le bracelet que j'avais perdu l'année dernière.

F. Vous êtes unique au monde! Your teacher is conducting a survey among his/her students. Answer the following questions so he/she can understand you better. (8 points)

1. Quels sont les avantages des grandes villes? _____

   _____

2. Où viviez-vous quand vous aviez cinq ans? _____

3. Savez-vous chanter? _____

4. Que faisiez-vous ce matin à 8h? _____

G. Le rendez-vous. Yesterday, your best friend Juliette was meeting her boyfriend in secret. To get the full story, fill in each blank with the correct tense of the verb in parentheses, either the **passé composé** or the **imparfait.** (16 points)

1. (aimer)   Autrefois, Juliette _____ Roméo.

2. (être)   Roméo, lui aussi, _____ très amoureux de Juliette.

3. (décider)   Un jour ils _____ d'aller faire un tour dans la forêt.

4. (regarder)   Tout d'un coup, Roméo _____ Juliette.

5. (faire)   Elle _____ de même *(the same thing)*.

6. (comprendre)   Soudain ils _____ leur chance.

7. (être)   Mais il _____ 11h du soir

8. (rentrer)   ... alors ils _____ tout de suite! (Le père de

   Juliette est très strict!)

H. Le dîner romantique de Roméo et Juliette. Roméo loves Juliette, so for her birthday he invited her to a very posh French restaurant, la Maison Robert. Something unpleasant happened during the dinner. (Use your imagination!) Describe their evening with at least six complete sentences. Supply as many details as possible and feel free to use expressions from the word bank, if you like. (18 points: 3 points per sentence, 2 points for accuracy of expression, and 1 point for richness of vocabulary)

arriver	finalement	une fois	d'habitude
longtemps	parfois	son portefeuille (*wallet*)	puis
le serveur	soudain		

Le dîner romantique de Roméo et Juliette

_____

_____

_____

_____

_____

_____

Unit Test 8B

A. Passé composé ou imparfait? You will hear five sentences. Listen to them carefully and then decide if each sentence is in the **passé composé** or the **imparfait.** (10 points)

	0	00	1	2	3	4	5
passé composé	✓						
imparfait		✓					

B. La vie en France. Listen to the following sentences on French culture. Listen carefully and then decide if each sentence is **vrai** (true) or **faux** (false). (12 points)

	0	1	2	3	4	5	6
vrai							
faux	✓						

C. Autrefois. Everyone likes to remember the "good old days." Answer the following questions about your childhood in complete sentences. (12 points)

1. _____

2. _____

3. _____

4. _____

D. Qui? Quoi? Comment? It's not who you know, it's what you know that counts. Complete each question below with either **Sais-tu** or **Connais-tu.** (8 points)

1. _____ personnellement le président des États-Unis?

2. _____ s'il parle français?

3. _____ un bon restaurant près du campus?

4. _____ à quelle heure il ferme?

E.   Un accident. There was an accident yesterday. To find out what happened, complete each sentence with either **qui, que,** or **qu'.** (8 points)

1.   Hier nous avons vu un accident _____ était horrible!

2.   C'est une scène _____ on ne va jamais oublier.

3.   Une voiture _____ allait très vite est rentrée dans un magasin.

4.   Le propriétaire *(owner)* _____ nous connaissons assez bien a été sérieusement blessé *(hurt)*.

F.   Vous êtes unique au monde! Your teacher is conducting a survey among his/students. Answer the following questions so he/she can understand you better. (16 points)

1.   Préférez-vous vivre en ville ou à la campagne? _____

_____

2.   Où vivez-vous maintenant? _____

3.   Savez-vous danser? _____

4.   Aviez-vous déjà étudié le français avant d'arriver à l'université? _____

_____

G.   La soucoupe volante. *(The UF0).* Yesterday, your best friend, Christophe, saw **une soucoupe volante** or **un OVNI** *(UFO).* To get the full story, fill in each blank with the correct tense of the verb in parentheses, either the **passé composé** or the **imparfait.** (16 points)

1.   (être)   Il _____ huit heures du soir.

2.   (faire)   Il _____ très beau.

3.   (sortir)   Après le dîner, Christophe _____ de sa maison.

4.   (voir)   Il _____ un objet lumineux à une distance de 100 mètres.

5.   (descendre)   Une étrange créature _____ de l'objet lumineux.

6.   (porter)   Elle _____ un costume vert et des antennes sur la tête.

7.   (prendre)   Christophe _____ deux photos de l'objet lumineux.

8.   (partir)   Puis l'objet lumineux _____ très vite avec son passager.

H. La fête de Fredy Fêtard. Fredy loves parties. Last weekend he had a party that ended badly. Describe the party with at least six complete sentences. Supply as many details as possible and feel free to use expressions from the word bank. (18 points: 3 points per sentence, 2 points for accuracy of expression, and 1 point for richness of vocabulary)

| avoir lieu | d'abord | un accident | alors | finalement |
| l'hôpital | pendant que | la police | tomber malade | tout à coup |

La fête de Fredy Fêtard

_____

_____

_____

_____

_____

_____

Unit Test 9A

A. Singulier ou pluriel? You will hear seven statements. Mark row one if the subject of the sentence is **singulier.** Mark row two if the subject of the sentence is **pluriel.** Mark row three if the subject of the sentence could be **singulier ou pluriel.** (14 points)

	0	00	1	2	3	4	5	6	7
singulier		✓							
pluriel									
singulier ou pluriel	✓								

B. La vie en France. You will hear six statements about French culture. Mark whether each statement is true **(vrai)** or false **(faux).** (12 points)

	0	1	2	3	4	5	6
vrai	✓						
faux							

C. Activités. Listen to what the following people have with them, and then say what they are doing, using an appropriate reflexive construction. (8 points)

MODEL:

0. **Je me brosse les dents.**

1. Tu _____

2. Ils _____

3. Elle _____

4. Nous _____

D. Suggestions et conseils. Tell the following people to do certain things. Use the **tu** or **vous** form, according to the context. (12 points)

MODEL:

0. **Couchez-vous!**

1. _____

2. _____

3. _____

4. _____

E. **De la tête aux pieds!** Choose the most logical answer to complete each sentence. (10 points)

1. Andrée a mal _____. Elle a mangé trop de chocolat.

   (a) au cœur   (b) au genou   (c) aux cheveux

2. Julie se peigne _____ après la douche.

   (a) les dents   (b) les cheveux   (c) les yeux

3. Beaucoup de joueurs de basket se rasent _____.

   (a) les pieds   (b) la tête   (c) les jambes

4. Arthur se lave souvent _____. Il est médecin.

   (a) le visage   (b) le nez   (c) les mains

5. Jeanne a mal _____. Elle a couru un marathon hier!

   (a) à la bouche   (b) aux pieds   (c) aux oreilles

F. **Hier.** Read what the following people are doing now. Say that they did these things yesterday, using the **passé composé.** (14 points)

MODEL:

0. Paul et Anne s'écrivent. __**Ils se sont écrit.**__

1. Marie et Philippe se rencontrent. _____

2. Je découvre la vérité. _____

3. Jacqueline s'amuse. _____

4. Émilie et Carole se perdent à Paris. _____

5. Nous nous donnons rendez-vous. _____

6. Vous vous parlez au téléphone. _____

7. Tu te mets en colère. _____

G. **Transformations.** Rewrite the sentences below, replacing the underlined words with object pronouns. (10 points)

1. Nous ne nous intéressons pas <u>au football américain</u>.

   _____

2. Est-ce que vous avez <u>des amis</u> en France?

   _____

3. J'ai pris un litre <u>d'eau</u>.

   _____

4. Marc et Henri vont passer la soirée <u>chez Chantal</u>.

_____

5. Achetons <u>du Perrier</u> pour la fête!

_____

H.   Dimanche matin. Ursule Fûté is a serious student and she has a huge crush on the librarian who works at the reference desk. Ursule always gets up early on Sunday mornings so she can be the first one to arrive at the library to study. Describe what happened to her last Sunday using at least five of the expressions in the word bank below. Be sure to use the **passé composé.** (20 points: 4 points per sentence, 3 points for accuracy of expression, and 1 point for richness of vocabulary)

découvrir	se dépêcher	s'habiller
porter le pantalon de son pyjama	se mettre en colère	se préparer
se rendre compte de	retourner chez elle	se tromper

Dimanche matin

_____

_____

_____

_____

_____

_____

Unit Test 9B

A. Singulier ou pluriel? You will hear seven statements. Mark row one if the subject of the sentence is **singulier.** Mark row two if the subject of the sentence is **pluriel.** Mark row three if the subject of the sentence could be **singulier ou pluriel.** (14 points)

	0	00	1	2	3	4	5	6	7
singulier									
pluriel		√							
singulier ou pluriel	√								

B. La vie en France. You will hear six statements about French culture. Mark whether each statement is true **(vrai)** or false **(faux).** (12 points)

	0	1	2	3	4	5	6
vrai	√						
faux							

C. Activités. Listen to what the following people have with them, and then say what they are doing, using an appropriate reflexive construction. (8 points)

MODEL:

0. Elle ____ **s'habille.** ____

1. Je _____

2. Nous _____

3. Tu _____

4. Vous _____

D. Suggestions et conseils. Tell the following people to do certain things. Use the **tu** or **vous** form, according to the context. (12 points)

MODEL:

0. **Fais des exercices.**

1. _____

2. _____

3. _____

4. _____

E. De la tête aux pieds! Choose the most logical answer to complete each sentence. (10 points)

1. Ses chaussures sont trop petites. Claire a mal _____.

   (a) aux yeux   (b) aux oreilles   (c) aux pieds

2. François a besoin d'aspirine. Il a mal _____.

   (a) à la tête   (b) au ventre   (c) au nez

3. Pierre est dentiste. Alors, il se brosse _____ après tous les repas.

   (a) les cheveux   (b) les dents   (c) le cœur

4. Martine a _____ verts.

   (a) les cheveux   (b) les doigts   (c) les yeux

5. Simon a _____ longs.

   (a) les cheveux   (b) les yeux   (c) le genou

F. Hier. Read what the following people are doing now. Say that they did these things yesterday, using the **passé composé.** (14 points)

MODEL:

0. Paul et Anne se téléphonent.   __**Ils se sont téléphoné.**__

1. Marc ouvre la fenêtre. _____

2. Sylvie court cinq kilomètres. _____

3. Tu te couches à minuit. _____

4. Nous nous réveillons à sept heures. _____

5. Fatima se promène en ville. _____

6. Pierre se lave les cheveux. _____

7. Je me trompe. _____

G. Transformations. Rewrite the sentences below, replacing the underlined words with object pronouns. (10 points)

1. Nicole n'a pas peur <u>de l'examen final.</u>

   _____

2. Est-ce que tu vas <u>au match de basket</u> ce soir?

   _____

3. Marc a acheté un kilo <u>de belles oranges.</u>

   _____

4. Tu n'as pas écrit ton nom <u>sur la liste</u>.

_____

5. Ne retournons jamais <u>dans ce restaurant!</u>

_____

H. Samedi soir. Fredy Fêtard usually has a great time on Saturday nights, but he is usually late _(en retard)_. Describe what happened to him last weekend using at least five of the expressions in the word bank. Be sure to use the **passé composé.** (20 points: 4 points per sentence, 3 points for accuracy of expression, and 1 point for richness of vocabulary)

s'amuser	arriver à l'heure _(on time)_	arriver en retard
donner rendez-vous	se disputer	s'énerver
s'excuser	se préoccuper	se rencontrer

Samedi soir

_____

_____

_____

_____

_____

_____

Aperçu culturel
La France, mère des arts (Version 9A)

A. Vrai ou faux? Read the following statements regarding the **Aperçu culturel** and decide whether they are true **(V)** or false **(F)**. (35 points)

_____ 1. La France a toujours eu une grande tradition artistique.

_____ 2. Pour voir des pièces d'art préhistorique, il faut aller au Louvre.

_____ 3. En général, l'art en France au Moyen Âge était religieux.

_____ 4. La Renaissance a commencé d'abord en France, puis en Italie.

_____ 5. Le règne de Louis XIV a été profondément marqué par l'art baroque.

_____ 6. Le romantisme du dix-neuvième siècle a touché la littérature et l'art.

_____ 7. L'impressionnisme a encouragé les peintres à reproduire les objets d'une façon très réaliste.

B. Qu'en savez-vous? Choose the answer that best completes each sentence. (35 points)

1. _____ a inspiré beaucoup de jeunes artistes vers la fin du dix-neuvième siècle.

   (a) Édouard Manet   (b) Paul Cézanne   (c) Berthe Morisot

2. *Impression, soleil levant* est un tableau de _____.

   (a) Vincent Van Gogh   (b) Pablo Picasso   (c) Claude Monet

3. Pour les impressionnistes, _____ jouait un rôle essentiel.

   (a) la couleur   (b) la perspective   (c) la religion

4. _____ étaient appelés des fauves à cause de leurs toiles aux couleurs violentes.

   (a) Matisse et Dufy   (b) Monet et Manet   (c) Magritte et Kandinsky

5. _____ ont été inspirés par les travaux de Freud.

   (a) Les impressionnistes   (b) Les fauvistes   (c) Les surréalistes

6. Avec _____ de l'art le rôle de la France dans le domaine artistique a changé.

   (a) l'internationalisation   (b) l'industrialisation   (c) la nationalisation

7. André Breton était à la tête du mouvement _____.

   (a) surréaliste   (b) impressionniste   (c) cubiste

C. La France, mere des arts. You are a time traveler and an art historian. Which era would you most like to visit? Why? (Your choices are **la Préhistoire, le Moyen Âge, la Renaissance** or **le commencement du vingtième siècle.**) (30 points: 20 points for accuracy, 10 points for development of ideas and vocabulary)

_____

_____

_____

_____

_____

_____

_____

_____

Aperçu culturel
La France, mère des arts (Version 9B)

A. Vrai ou faux? Read the following statements regarding the **Aperçu culturel** and decide whether they are true (**V**) or false (**F**). (35 points)

_____ 1. Les Français visitent régulièrement les musées parce qu'ils sont passionnés par l'art.

_____ 2. L'histoire de l'art en France commence au Moyen Âge.

_____ 3. Aujourd'hui, il est difficile de trouver des pièces d'art médiéval en France.

_____ 4. François 1er a beaucoup fait pour le développement de l'art en France.

_____ 5. Louis XIV le «Roi Soleil» est responsable de l'architecture grandiose du dix-septième siècle.

_____ 6. Versailles représente bien l'âge classique.

_____ 7. Au vingtième siècle des artistes étrangers comme Picasso, Modigliani et Chagall sont venus vivre en France.

B. Qu'en savez-vous? Choose the answer that best completes each sentence. (35 points)

1. _____ ont joué avec la lumière et la couleur dans leurs tableaux.

   (a) Les impressionnistes   (b) Les fauves   (c) Les surréalistes

2. Au début, le public a été _____ par les nouveaux styles d'art comme l'impressionisme, le

   fauvisme et le surréalisme.

   (a) enthousiasmé   (b) intéressé   (c) choqué

3. Paul Gauguin était un peintre _____.

   (a) impressionniste   (b) post-impressionniste   (c) cubiste

4. Le fauvisme, le cubisme et l'art abstrait font partie _____.

   (a) de l'art classique   (b) du romantisme   (c) de l'art moderne

5. Dali et Magritte sont des _____ très connus.

   (a) surréalistes   (b) impressionnistes   (c) cubistes

6. Les surréalistes aiment explorer _____.

   (a) le monde réel   (b) l'inconscient (the subconcious)   (c) la couleur et la lumière

7. Pour les Français, il est important que l'art soit accessible _____.

   (a) à tout le monde   (b) aux grands artistes   (c) aux bourgeois

C. L'art et l'artiste. Imagine you are a famous painter living in France during one of the following eras: **le Moyen Âge, la Renaissance, l'âge classique, l'âge romantique** or **le vingtième siècle.** Say who you are and when you lived, and describe your art. What motivates you to create? (**Quelles sont vos motivations? la religion? la politique? vos émotions?**) What are your favorite subjects to paint? Why? (30 points: 20 points for accuracy, 10 points for development of ideas and vocabulary)

_____

_____

_____

_____

_____

_____

_____

_____

_____

NOM _____ CLASSE _____ DATE _____

Unit Test 10A

A. La rencontre. A mutual friend, Véronique Fournier, decides to introduce Pierre and Chantal to one another because they have a lot in common and she thinks they will get along well. Listen to the story of how they meet and fill in the blanks with the word you hear. (21 points: 1 point per adverb 2 points per question)

Véronique a donné rendez-vous à Pierre pour 4h au café parisien La Coupole. Elle lui a dit qu'elle

a une amie qui vient avec elle. Pierre arrive _____ à 4h et cherche partout

mais Véronique et son amie ne sont pas là. Il s'assied, commande un café crème et il les attend

_____. Enfin, à 4h30 les deux filles arrivent. Véronique s'excuse et

elle explique qu'_____ elles avaient raté leur bus. Pierre lui répond

_____ que ça va. Alors, Véronique les présente l'un à l'autre et tout

le monde s'assied. Véronique commence à parler _____ d'un film

qu'elle vient de voir mais les deux autres sont timides et ils ne disent rien. Mais quand Véronique dit

une bêtise *(something stupid)* au sujet du film, Chantal, qui est une grande cinéphile, commence à

donner ses opinions personnelles. Elle discute _____ de la

cinématographie. Pierre l'écoute _____ et il commence, alors,

à s'intéresser à cette fille intelligente.

And now, answer the following questions.

1. Est-ce que Pierre arrive à l'heure? _____ Oui _____ Non (Comment le savez-vous?) _____

    _____

2. Pourquoi est-ce que Véronique et Chantal arrivent en retard? _____

    _____

3. Est-ce que Pierre est fâché quand les filles arrivent enfin? _____ Oui _____ Non (Expliquez.)

    _____

4. Est-ce que Véronique sait quelque chose sur le cinéma? _____ Oui _____ Non (Expliquez.)

    _____

Test Sheets: Unit Test 10A **TP** **97**

5. Et Chantal en sait-elle quelque chose? _____ Oui _____ Non (Expliquez.)

_____

6. Est-ce que Pierre parle trop? _____ Oui _____ Non (Expliquez.)

_____

7. Est-ce que Pierre s'intéresse à Chantal? _____ Oui _____ Non

   Pourquoi ou pourquoi pas? _____

   _____

B. La vie en France. Pierre et Chantal are typically French in their opinions about marriage, careers, mobility, and vacations. Based upon your knowledge of French customs and attitudes found in the *Notes culturelles*, indicate whether the following statements are **vrai** or **faux.** (12 points)

	0	1	2	3	4	5	6
vrai	✓						
faux							

C. L'immeuble de Chantal. Pierre stops by Chantal's apartment building and notices the mailboxes. As you hear each apartment number, fill in the corresponding floor on your answer sheet. For example, apartment 328 would be on the third floor. (12 points)

MODEL:

0. Les Neis habitent au ___**septième**___ étage.

1. Les Fabre habitent au _____ étage.

2. Chantal habite au _____ étage.

3. Les Guérin habitent au _____ étage.

4. Les Saint Martin habitent au _____ étage.

5. Les Verdier habitent au _____ étage.

6. Les Perez habitent au _____ étage.

C. Au contraire! Michel has strong opinions about everything, as do you. Listen to his ideas and then write the opposite, beginning your sentences with the expressions below. (12 points)

1. Je doute que _____ _____.

2. Je ne pense pas que _____.

3. Je ne suis pas sûr(e) qu'_____.

4. Il n'est pas vrai que _____.

D. Questions personnelles. You will hear five questions. Listen to them carefully and then answer them in complete sentences. Write only the answers. (15 points)

1. _____

2. _____

3. _____

4. _____

5. _____

E. Des conseils. Your cousin, Theo, is going to college in the fall. He looks to you for advice on how to succeed during that crucial first year. Use items from the chart below to make useful suggestions. Do not use any item twice. (18 points)

MODEL:

Il est important / assister aux cours.   You would write: **Il est important que tu assistes aux cours.**

Il faut que	aller à beaucoup de fêtes
Il est essentiel que	être sérieux
Il vaut mieux que	étudier beaucoup
Je souhaite que	dormir toute la journée
Je sais que	se faire des amis
J'ai peur que	suivre des cours intéressants

1. _____

2. _____

3. _____

4. _____

5. _____

6. _____

Unit Test 11A

A. Avant de partir. Madame Javert and her husband, Jean, live in Vermont and are traveling to Québec this summer. She is a worrier and he is very demanding. Listen to the message she left on her best friend's answering machine and fill in the blanks with the word you hear. (14 points: 1 point per missing verb and 1 point per **vrai/faux** item)

Salut, Sophie! C'est Andrée. Je ne sais pas quoi faire! Il faut que je _____ tellement

de choses avant de partir en vacances. D'abord mon mari veut que je _____ des

places sur un vol d'Air Canada. Bien sûr, il faut que ces places _____ bon marché!

Donc, il faut que j'_____ chez l'agent de voyage ou peut-être que je trouverais ça

sur Internet. Qui sait? Il est aussi essentiel que nous _____ logés dans un hôtel

moderne. Il est nécessaire que notre hôtel _____ tous les conforts! En plus, il est

possible que notre chat, Einstein, _____ avec nous. Alors, il est essentiel que

nous _____ trouver un hôtel qui accepte les animaux. Il n'est pas sûr qu'on

en trouve un. Et puis, je ne pense pas que nous _____ besoin de nos passeports.

Sais-tu si on en a besoin? Je veux que tu me _____ tout de suite pour me donner

des conseils! À bientôt!

Reread the preceding paragraph and then decide whether the following statements are **vrai** or **faux.**

_____ 1. Madame Javert n'est pas très occupée actuellement.

_____ 2. Les Javert ne font pas très attention à leur budget.

_____ 3. Il leur faut un hôtel moderne et confortable.

_____ 4. Il faut absolument qu'ils aient des passeports pour aller au Canada.

_____ 5. Il vaut mieux qu'ils trouvent un hôtel qui accepte les animaux.

B. Les Québécois, les Européens et la technologie. Listen to the following statements regarding Québec, Europe, and technology in France, and decide whether they are **vrai** or **faux.** (14 points)

	0	1	2	3	4	5	6	7
vrai								
faux	✓							

Unit Test 10B

A. La cérémonie. The groom and all the guests have already arrived at the town hall and are anxiously awaiting the bride-to-be. **Les témoins** *(the witnesses)* and **le maire** *(the mayor)* are there as well. Listen to find out what happened before the ceremony began. Fill in the blanks with the word you hear. (23 points: 1 point per adverb, 2 points per question)

Marc est arrivé en avance comme d'habitude et _____ Élodie est en retard.

Marc est très déçu. Pourtant, la cérémonie doit commencer dans un instant. Marc regarde sa montre

_____. Il lui avait bien dit 16h, il se dit _____.

À 16h15 il commence à s'inquiéter. Il se demande _____ si Élodie n'a pas

changé d'avis. Elle lui avait dit plusieurs fois qu'elle voulait _____ passer le

reste de sa vie avec lui. Mais depuis deux semaines elle parle souvent de son nouveau voisin, Bob.

Bob est américain. C'est un bel homme sportif qui passe six mois aux États-Unis et six mois en France.

Marc a remarqué que quand Bob parle elle l'écoute toujours très _____.

Est-ce l'amour ou _____ son joli accent américain qu'elle apprécie? Mais

_____ Marc aperçoit la mariée qui arrive. Elle le regarde

_____ et _____. La cérémonie peut commencer.

And now, answer the following questions.

1. En général, est-ce que Marc est ponctuel? (Expliquez.) _____

    _____

2. Marc est assez nerveux. Comment le remarque-t-on? _____

    _____

3. Qu'est-ce qu'Élodie a dit pour montrer qu'elle aimait beaucoup Marc?

    _____

4. Pourquoi est-ce que Marc pense qu'elle ne veut plus se marier avec lui?

    _____

5. Marc croit qu'Élodie s'intéresse au voisin, Bob?

    _____

6. Comment sait-on qu'Élodie veut épouser Marc à la fin de l'histoire?

   _____

7. Est-ce que Marc et Élodie se marient à la fin de l'histoire? _____

   _____

B. La vie en France. Marc and Élodie are typically French in their opinions about marriage, careers, mobility, and vacations. Based upon your knowledge of French customs and attitudes found in the *Notes culturelles,* indicate whether the following statements are **vrai** or **faux.** (12 points)

	0	1	2	3	4	5	6
vrai							
faux	✓						

C. Les faire-part *(The Invitations).* Several weeks before the wedding, Élodie and Marc prepare the invitations to be mailed. All of their friends live in Paris, but in different **arrondissements.** The last two digits of each zip code indicate **l'arrondissement.** Listen to the zip code and then write which **arrondissement** the guests live in. (12 points)

MODEL:

  0. Les Laforgue habitent dans le ___**quatorzième**___ arrondissement.

  1. Les Fabre habitent dans le _____ arrondissement.

  2. Chantal et Robert habitent dans le _____ arrondissement.

  3. Michel Martin habite dans le _____ arrondissement.

  4. Les Saintonge habitent dans le _____ arrondissement.

  5. Isabelle et Jacques Van Mol habitent dans le _____ arrondissement.

  6. Marie-Pierre Bouchez habite dans le _____ arrondissement.

D. La lune de miel. Élodie has written the following postcard to a friend about the honeymoon she and Marc have planned. Fill in the blanks with the proper **future** form of the correct verb from the verb bank below. (18 points)

aller   avoir   courir   envoyer
faire   partir   pouvoir   vouloir

Chère Carole,

Nous avons décidé; nous _____ en Guadeloupe en lune de miel. Nous _____ de Paris le 25 juin. Là-bas nous _____ des promenades romantiques sur les belles plages. Pendant notre séjour, il y _____ un festival de musique zouk.

On _____ aussi connaître la cuisine des îles.

Je t'_____ une carte postale!

Amitiés,

Élodie

Mlle. MAJOUX Carole
11, rue de l'Aigle
COMPIÈGNE 60200

E. Au téléphone. Élodie and Marc have just finished their university studies. Élodie is a journalist and already has a job offer to work for *Libération,* a Paris-based newspaper. Marc would like to move to the country and start a family. He dreams of having a vineyard in Provence. During a phone conversation one afternoon, they discuss their different options. Complete their dialogue by choosing the appropriate verb tense from the choices given. (10 points)

ÉLODIE: Où veux-tu qu'on habite plus tard? Dans quel arrondissement?

MARC::   Je ne sais pas. Si on allait vivre en Provence, on _____ (1) une vie beaucoup plus calme. Tu ne trouves pas?

      (a) aurai   (b) avais   (c) aurait

ÉLODIE: Oui, mais dans le journalisme, tout se passe à Paris!

MARC::   Oui, tu as raison. Mais, si nous _____ (2) en Provence, nous pourrions fonder une famille tout de suite!

      (a) vivions   (b) vivrions   (c) vivrons

ÉLODIE: Mais la Provence est trop loin de Paris, je te dis.

MARC::   Et moi? Si on vit à Paris, qu'est-ce que je _____ (3)?

      (a) faisait   (b) ferai   (c) ferais

ÉLODIE: Si j'_____ (4) le choix, je chercherais du travail en Provence, mais je n'ai pas le choix.

      (a) avais   (b) ai   (c) aurai

MARC::   Et si j'étais à ta place, je _____ (5) content d'aller vivre au soleil!

      (a) suis   (b) serais   (c) serai

F.   Composition guidée. Imaginez que vous vous mariez. Que feriez-vous avant la cérémonie? Seriez-vous nerveux (nerveuse)? Pourquoi ou pourquoi pas? (25 points: 20 points for accuracy of expression, 5 points for imagination and vocabulary)

_____

_____

_____

_____

_____

_____

_____

_____

F. Composition guidée. Imaginez que vous vivez en France. Comment serait votre vie? Seriez-vous heureux (heureuse)? Pourquoi ou pourquoi pas? (25 points: 20 points for accuracy of expression, 5 points for imagination and vocabulary)

_____

_____

_____

_____

_____

_____

_____

_____

D. La carte postale. Chantal has written the following postcard to a friend about her summer plans. Fill in the blanks with the proper **future** form of the correct verb from the verb bank below. (15 points)

aller	avoir	courir	durer
faire	pouvoir	recevoir	voir

Bonjour Martine!

J'ai fait la connaissance d'un garçon qui s'appelle Pierre.

Il est vraiment sympa. Quand tu me rendras visite en juin, tu

_____ qu'il est très beau! Nous

_____ des matches de tennis ensemble. Est-ce

que tu aimes le jazz? Nous _____ l'occasion

d'assister au Festival de musique à Aix-en-Provence si ça

t'intéresse. Le Festival _____ tout le mois de

juin. J'ai une voiture, donc *(therefore)* je _____

conduire, si tu veux.

Amitiés,

Chantal

Mlle. AUBRAC Martine
11, rue de l'Aigle
COMPIÈGNE 60200

E. Au téléphone. Since Pierre and Chantal are nearing the end of their college careers, they are having a life crisis. During a phone conversation one afternoon, they begin to discuss their different options. Complete their dialogue by choosing the appropriate verb tense from the choices given. (15 points)

CHANTAL: Qu'est-ce que tu vas faire après l'université?

PIERRE: Je ne sais pas. Si je continuais mes études, je n'_____ (1) pas besoin de prendre cette décision maintenant.

(a) aurai   (b) avais   (c) aurais

CHANTAL: Oui, mais il est nécessaire de gagner de l'argent.

PIERRE: Oui, tu as raison. Si mon père _____ (2) riche, je ne travaillerais pas.

(a) avait   (b) était   (c) étaient

CHANTAL: Mais ton père n'est pas riche.

PIERRE: C'est bien vrai, mais s'il gagne à la loterie, tout _____ (3).

(a) change   (b) changerait   (c) changera

CHANTAL: Tu rêves! Si j'_____ (4) besoin d'argent, je chercherai du travail tout de suite.

(a) avais   (b) ai   (c) suis

PIERRE: Et si j'étais à ta place, je _____ (5) moins sérieuse.

(a) suis   (b) serais   (c) serai

F. Le Canada et les États-Unis. Complete the following sentences about our relationship with Canada by choosing the most logical answer in each case. (4 points)

1. En général, nous avons de bons _____ avec nos voisins du nord.

    (a) amis   (b) problèmes   (c) rapports

2. Les Canadiens étaient nos _____ pendant les deux guerres mondiales.

    (a) alliés   (b) citoyens   (c) ennemis

3. Nous _____ une frontière avec eux.

    (a) menaçons   (b) partageons   (c) organisons

4. Quand un étranger veut visiter le Canada, il faut qu'il passe _____.

    (a) par la douane   (b) au supermarché   (c) à la banque

G. Tous les pronoms du monde. Answer the following questions, replacing the underlined words with pronouns. Watch out as some answers require two pronouns! (14 points)

MODEL:

Donnez-vous souvent <u>des cadeaux</u> <u>à vos parents</u>?   **Oui, je leur en donne souvent.**

1. Prêtez-vous <u>vos CDs</u> <u>à vos amis</u>?

    _____

2. Est-ce que vous <u>vous</u> servez souvent <u>d'un ordinateur</u>?

    _____

3. Envoyez-vous souvent <u>des e-mails</u> <u>à votre meilleur(e) ami(e)</u>?

    _____

4. Est-ce qu'il y a <u>des étudiants étrangers</u> dans votre classe de français?

    _____

5. Est-ce que vous <u>vous</u> intéressez <u>à la politique</u>?

    _____

H. Aimez-vous les cadeaux? Your professor is in a generous mood. He/she offers you the following items. Respond negatively or affirmatively using the imperative form according to the model. The underlined words must be replaced by object pronouns. (9 points)

MODEL:

Je peux <u>vous</u> donner <u>des livres de poésie</u>?   **Oui, donnez-m'en!**

1. Je peux <u>vous</u> donner <u>ma BMW noire</u>?

   _____

2. Je peux <u>vous</u> offrir <u>ma collection de CDs des années 70</u>?

   _____

3. Je peux <u>vous</u> prêter <u>de l'argent</u>?

   _____

Unit Test 11B

A. Vive la France profonde! Your French grandfather is not in favor of the European Union; his father fought in World War II. He left this message on your answering machine because he thinks there is hope for you yet. Listen to the message and fill in the blanks with the missing verb that you hear. (14 points: 1 point per missing verb and 1 point per **vrai/faux** item)

Bonjour, Laure. Comment vas-tu? C'est Pépé. Il faut que je te parle. J'ai peur qu'on _____

notre identité française. Il est préférable que nous _____ l'Union européenne

pour qu'on _____ nos bonnes traditions. Je doute qu'on _____

se sentir français et européen. En plus, il n'est pas vrai que tout le monde _____

une monnaie unique. Je sais que l'Allemagne et l'Angleterre sont nos alliées à l'heure actuelle, mais je

déplore qu'elles _____ autant d'influence sur notre beau pays. Il faut absolument

qu'on _____ quelque chose avant qu'il _____ trop tard!

Crois-tu que la France _____ les risques de sa politique européenne? Moi, je n'en

suis pas très sûr. Rappelle-moi vite, ma belle, pour continuer cette discussion importante.

Reread the preceding paragraph and then decide whether each statement is **vrai** or **faux.**

_____ 1. Le grand-père de Laure n'est pas vraiment en faveur de l'Union européenne.

_____ 2. Il ne se sent pas français et européen.

_____ 3. Il pense que l'Union européenne a une influence négative sur la France.

_____ 4. Il croit qu'il faut s'intéresser à la situation de la France tout de suite.

_____ 5. Il est certain que les Français comprennent la situation actuelle.

B. Les Québécois, les Européens et la technologie. Listen to the following statements regarding Québec, Europe, and technology in France, and decide whether they are true or false. (14 points)

	0	1	2	3	4	5	6	7
vrai								
faux	✓							

C. Au contraire! Michèle has strong opinions about everything, as do you. Listen to her ideas and then write the opposite, beginning your sentences with the expressions below. (12 points)

1. Je ne crois pas que _____

2. Il est douteux que _____

3. Je ne suis pas certain(e) _____

4. Je ne suis pas surpris(e) qu'_____

D. Questions personnelles. You will hear five questions. Listen to them carefully and then answer them in complete sentences. Write only the answer. (15 points)

1. _____

2. _____

3. _____

4. _____

5. _____

E. Des conseils. Your cousin, Caitlin, is going to work in Montréal for the summer to improve her French. She looks to you for advice on how to make the most of her experience. Use items from the chart below to make useful suggestions. Do not use any item twice. (18 points)

MODEL:

Il faut que / suivre des cours de conversation

You would write: **Il faut que tu suives des cours de conversation.**

Il est préférable que	pouvoir utiliser son français
Il est important que	vouloir aller à Montréal
Il est indispensable que	se faire des amis francophones
Je suis fier (fière) que	être à l'heure au travail
Je suis content(e) que	aller voir des films français
Je veux que	partir au Québec cet été

1. _____

2. _____

3. _____

4. _____

5. _____

6. _____

F. Vive le progrès! Complete the following sentences by choosing the most logical answer in each case. (4 points)

1. Microsoft Word et Windows 2000 sont _____.

   (a) des logiciels   (b) des appareils   (c) des découvertes récentes

2. Si on _____ d'un ordinateur, tout va plus vite, en principe.

   (a) se passe   (b) se sert   (c) s'occupe

3. Pierre et Marie Curie étaient de grands _____ français.

   (a) chefs   (b) écrivains   (c) savants

4. Une cure pour le SIDA *(AIDS)* serait _____ très importante.

   (a) une découverte   (b) une invention   (c) un moyen

G. Tous les pronoms du monde. Answer the following questions, replacing the underlined words with pronouns. Attention! Some answers require two pronouns. (14 points)

MODEL:

   Est-ce que je <u>vous</u> donne souvent <u>de bonnes notes</u>?   **Oui, vous nous en donnez souvent.**

1. Est-ce que vous <u>me</u> prêtez <u>de l'argent</u>? _____

2. Écrivez-vous souvent <u>des lettres</u> <u>à vos parents</u>? _____

3. Aimeriez-vous être <u>le(la) président(e) des États-Unis?</u>

   _____

4. Y a-t-il parfois <u>des films français</u> qui jouent au cinéma de votre ville? _____

   _____

5. Avez-vous <u>des amis</u> au Québec? _____

H. Vous vous y intéressez? Your best friend wants to find you a boyfriend or girlfriend. He/she just happens to know quite a few famous people. Listen to his/her suggestions and answer affirmatively or negatively with the imperative form and the appropriate pronouns. (9 points)

MODEL:

   Je peux envoyer ta photo à Adam Sandler (Kate Moss)?   **Non, ne la lui envoie pas.**

1. Je peux donner <u>ton numéro de téléphone</u> <u>à Ricky Martin</u> (<u>à Halle Berry</u>)?

   _____

2. Je peux <u>te</u> présenter <u>Johnny Dep et Keanu Reeves</u> (<u>Elizabeth Hurley et Janet Jackson</u>)?

   _____

3. Je peux donner <u>ton adresse électronique</u> <u>à M. C. Solaar</u> (<u>à Juliette Binoche</u>)?

   _____

UNIT TEST ANSWER KEY

Unit Test 1A

A. Qui est-ce?
1. Besson
2. Modiano
3. Bonnaire
4. Depardieu
5. Ledoyen
6. Binoche

B. Une lettre.

Cher John,

Salut! Comment <u>ça va</u>? Je <u>vais</u> <u>comme</u> <u>ci</u> <u>comme</u> <u>ça</u>. J'habite à <u>Paris</u>, mais je ne suis pas <u>français</u>. Je suis <u>algérien</u>. J'aime <u>bien</u> la musique <u>américaine</u>, mais je <u>préfère</u> le raï parce que c'est une musique <u>algérienne</u>. Je <u>n'aime</u> <u>pas</u> tellement les films romantiques. Je <u>déteste</u> le Front national. Et toi?

À <u>bientôt</u>!

Amitiés,
Moustafa

C. Bonjour! (*Exact answers for "A." Sample answers for "B."*)
1. A) Bonjour, Sophie. Ça va?
   B) Oui, ça va très bien.
2. A) Édouard, je te présente ma copine, Élisabeth.
   B) Bonjour, Elizabeth. OR Enchanté.
3. A) Comment vous appelez-vous?
   B) Je m'appelle...
4. A) Merci, Christine.
   B) De rien.

D. Et vous? (*Sample answers; answers will vary.*)
1. américain(e)
2. pas mal
3. Matt Dillon
4. Madonna
5. Kid Rock
6. New York

E. Une question de nationalité.
1. français
2. québécoise
3. anglais
4. américaine

F. Géographie.
1. la Martinique
2. la Guadeloupe
3. Saint-Pierre-et-Miquelon
4. la Polynésie française

G. Aperçu culturel: Vrai ou faux.
1. V
2. V
3. F
4. F
5. F
6. V
7. F
8. F
9. V
10. F

Unit Test 1B

A. Qui est-ce?
1. Bussières
2. Bouchez
3. Auteuil
4. Huppert
5. Reno
6. Veber

B. Une lettre.

Chère Britney,

Salut! Comment <u>vas-tu</u>? Je <u>vais</u> <u>bien</u>. J'habite à <u>Fort-de-France</u>; c'est à la <u>Martinique</u>. Je suis <u>martiniquaise</u>. J'adore la musique <u>américaine</u> et la musique <u>française</u>. J'<u>aime</u> <u>bien</u> les concerts et le cinéma. Je <u>préfère</u> le cinéma <u>français</u>. Je <u>n'aime</u> <u>pas</u> tellement le sport. Je <u>déteste</u> la violence et le racisme. Et toi?

À <u>bientôt</u>.

Bien amicalement,
Simone

C. Bonjour! (*Exact answers for "A." Sample answers for "B."*)
1. A) Bonjour, je m'appelle Sophie. Et toi?
   B) Je m'appelle...
2. A) Oui, ça va bien. Et toi?
   B) Ça va comme ci comme ça.
3. A) Bonjour. Je vous présente mon ami, Pierre.
   B) Enchanté(e).
4. A) Au revoir, Jean-Paul.
   B) Au revoir. À bientôt.

D. Et vous? (*Sample answers; answers will vary.*)
1. très bien
2. américain(e)
3. Santana
4. *Who Wants To Be a Millionaire?*
5. Jean-Claude Van Damme
6. Burger King

E. Une question de nationalité.
1. anglais 3. française
2. américaine 4. américain

F. Géographie. (*Answers may vary.*)
1. la Guyane française
2. la Guadeloupe
3. la Martinique
4. la Polynésie française (Tahiti)

G. Aperçu culturel: Vrai ou faux.

1. V	5. F	8. V
2. F	6. V	9. V
3. V	7. F	10. V
4. F		

Unit Test 2A

A. Visitons les pays francophones!

1. c	3. a	5. b
2. d	4. b	

B. Quelle heure est-il?

1. D	3. A	5. C
2. E	4. F	

C. Trois amies.

1. P	3. I	5. P
2. P	4. S	6. S

D. Mathieu.

1. 20	3. 192	5. 35
2. 19	4. 13	

E. La réponse est non!
1. Je n'aime pas écouter le rap.
2. Ils ne sont pas au Canada.
3. Vous ne voyagez pas beaucoup.
4. Tu ne parles pas bien français.
5. Nous n'arrivons pas à 22h.

F. Questions personnelles. (*Sample answers; answers will vary.*)
1. Nous sommes mercredi.
2. J'arrive à l'université à 9 heures.
3. Je regarde *Ally McBeal* le lundi.
4. J'habite avec deux camarades.
5. Oui, j'aime voyager.
6. J'étudie le soir et le week-end.

G. Culture.

1. F	6. V	11. V
2. F	7. F	12. V
3. V	8. V	13. V
4. F	9. V	14. V
5. V	10. F	15. F

Unit Test 2B

A. Visitons les pays francophones!

1. b	3. d	5. c
2. a	4. a	

B. Quelle heure est-il?

1. B	3. A	5. D
2. C	4. E	

C. Trois amis.

1. I	3. S	5. S
2. P	4. P	6. I

D. La vie de Christine.

1. 19	3. 95	5. 47
2. 23	4. 72	

E. La réponse est non!
1. Vous ne chantez pas bien.
2. Je ne suis pas à Montréal.
3. Pierre n'invite pas Paul.
4. Roméo n'aime pas regarder Juliette.
5. Tu ne regardes pas souvent la télé.

F. Questions personnelles. (*Sample answers; answers will vary.*)
1. C'est le 12 octobre.
2. Nous sommes lundi.
3. Je m'appelle...
4. J'habite à...
5. Oui, j'aime danser.
6. Oui, je suis américain(e).

G. Culture.

1. V	6. V	11. V
2. V	7. V	12. F
3. V	8. V	13. F
4. F	9. V	14. F
5. V	10. F	15. V

Unit Test 3A

A. Des amis.

1. I	3. M	5. M
2. F	4. I	

B. Logique ou illogique?

1. L	3. I	5. I
2. I	4. L	

C. Une chambre d'étudiant(e).
1. Oui, il y a une guitare.
2. Oui, il y a un lecteur de CD-ROM.
3. Non, il n'y a pas de moto.

4. Oui, il y a un téléphone.
5. Non, il n'y pas de caméscope.

D. Demain aussi.
1. Nathalie va utiliser son ordinateur.
2. nous allons jouer aux échecs.
3. vous allez étudier les maths.
4. tu vas passer des heures à la bibliothèque.
5. Anne et Sophie vont visiter Paris.

E. Questions personnelles. (*Sample answers; answers will vary.*)
1. Oui, j'aime voyager.
2. Non, je ne vais pas souvent au supermarché.
3. Oui, il y a une télévision dans ma chambre.
4. Je préfère voyager en voiture.
5. Oui, j'ai beaucoup de cousins.

F. Vous êtes sophistiqué(e).
1. Voici une copine brillante.
2. Voici des professeurs patients.
3. Voici un bon ordinateur.
4. Voici de jolies voitures.
5. Voici un mauvais café.

G. Lettre à un copain.
Cher Olivier,
   Ma cousine s'appelle Christine. Comment est-elle? <u>Elle est</u> très intelligente, mais <u>c'est</u> une fille très timide. Elle joue <u>du</u> piano, mais elle ne joue pas très bien. Elle adore <u>l'</u>art et elle va souvent <u>au</u> musée avec moi. <u>Elle est</u> très sophistiquée. Elle a beaucoup d'amis, mais <u>c'est</u> une personne égoïste...
Amitiés,
Jean-Michel

H. Vous avez une opinion? (*Sample answers; answers may vary slightly.*)

Bonnes qualités
Elle est très intelligente.
Elle adore l'art.
Elle est très sophistiquée.
Elle a beaucoup d'amis.

Mauvaises qualités
Elle est très timide.
Elle ne joue pas très bien du piano.
Elle est égoïste.

(Whether the student thinks that Jean-Michel will or won't like Christine is a matter of opinion.)

I. Une question de culture.
1. V   4. F   7. F
2. F   5. V   8. F
3. F   6. V

Unit Test 3B

A. Des amis.
1. I   3. I   5. M
2. I   4. F

B. Logique ou illogique?
1. I   3. L   5. L
2. I   4. I

C. Une chambre d'étudiante(e).
1. Non, il n'y a pas de cassettes.
2. Non, il n'y a pas d'appareil-photo.
3. Non, il n'y a pas de vélo.
4. Oui, il y a un ordinateur.
5. Oui, il y a une radio.

D. Demain aussi.
1. tu vas passer chez Marc.
2. Éric va jouer du piano.
3. mes amis vont voyager en train.
4. nous allons rester chez nous.
5. vous allez jouer aux cartes.

E. Questions personnelles. (*Sample answers; answers will vary.*)
1. Oui, j'aime la musique.
2. Non, je n'ai pas de camarade de chambre.
3. Oui, j'ai un vélo.
4. Je vais à la bibliothèque à pied.
5. Je rentre chez moi en avion.

F. Vous êtes sophistiqué(e)!
1. Voici une femme mariée.
2. Voici une fille heureuse.
3. Voici une grande piscine.
4. Voici un garçon timide.
5. Voici des étudiants américains.
6. Voici de jolies montres.

G. Lettre à une amie.
Chère Jeannette,
   Mon cousin s'appelle Jean-Michel. Comment est-il? <u>C'est</u> un garçon très dynamique. En général, <u>il est</u> très amusant, mais <u>c'est</u> un garçon pénible quand il n'est pas content. Il joue très bien <u>de la</u> guitare. Il adore <u>le</u> sport et il joue souvent <u>au</u> volley avec moi. Si je joue bien, <u>il est</u> très désagréable...
Amitiés,
Christine

H. Vous avez une opinion?

Bonnes qualités
Il est dynamique et amusant.
Il joue très bien de la guitare.
Il adore le sport.

Mauvaises qualités
Il est pénible.
Il est désagréable.

(Whether the student thinks that Jeannette will or won't like Jean-Michel is a matter of opinion.)

I. Une question de culture.

1. F	4. V	7. V
2. F	5. V	8. F
3. F	6. F	

Unit Test 4A

A. Le budget de Dominique.
loyer: 365 euros   bourse: 172 euros
transports: 39 euros   téléphone: 27 euros
loisirs: 164 euros

B. Dans la maison.

1. b	3. c
2. a	4. a

C. Une question de culture.

1. V	3. V	5. V
2. F	4. F	

D. Possessions.

1. notre	3. leur	5. ta
2. vos	4. son	6. son

E. Activités.
1. Nous faisons des économies.
2. Mes soeurs nettoient leur(s) chambre(s).
3. Sophie achète un anorak.
4. Tu paies le loyer.
5. Vous faites une promenade.

F. Comparaisons personnelles.
1. Une voiture est plus chère qu'un vélo.
2. Je suis plus jeune (moins jeune) que mon (ma) meilleur(e) ami(e).
3. La pièce la plus confortable est le salon. (Answers will vary.)

G. Vêtements. (*Answers will vary.*)
Elle porte un joli pull bleu et une longue jupe noire. Elle porte des lunettes noires. Elle porte des bottes marron. Elle porte des bas. Elle porte une veste bleue.

H. Une chambre d'étudiant(e).

1. b	3. b
2. a	4. c

Unit Test 4B

A. Le budget d'Isabelle.
loyer: 546 euros   salaire: 2.286 euros
vêtements: 182 euros   Internet: 30 euros
repas: 65 euros

B. Dans la maison.

1. b	3. c
2. c	4. a

C. Une question de culture.

1. V	3. F	5. V
2. V	4. F	

D. Possessions.

1. leur	3. ses	5. son
2. votre	4. ton	

E. Activités.
1. Nous gagnons de l'argent.
2. Mes frères font leurs devoirs.
3. Monique répète sa leçon.
4. Tu achètes un ordinateur.
5. Vous louez une maison à Nice.

F. Comparaisons personnelles. (*Answers may vary for questions 2 and 3.*)
1. Un appartement est moins cher qu'une maison.
2. Je dépense plus (moins) que mon (ma) camarade de chambre.
3. La meilleure saison est l'été.

G. Vêtements. (*Answers will vary.*)
Il porte une chemise blanche avec une cravate bleue. Il porte une belle veste noire. Il porte un nouveau pantalon marron. Il porte des lunettes noires.

H. Une chambre d'étudiant(e). (*Answers will vary.*)
1. Le lit est près de la fenêtre.
2. L'ordinateur est sur le bureau.
3. Les chaussures sont sous le lit.
4. Le téléphone est près de l'ordinateur.

Unit Test 5A

A. Dates historiques.

1. 1429	3. 1793	5. 1610
2. 1804	4. 1223	

B. Voyage au présent ou voyage au passé?

1. PC	3. PC	5. P
2. PC	4. P	6. PC

C. **Combien?**
1. P   3. S   5. P
2. S   4. S

D. **Une question de culture.**
1. F   3. V   5. F
2. F   4. V

E. **Hier aussi.**
1. a attendu ses copains.
2. avons rencontré nos amis.
3. a plu.
4. êtes parti(e)(s) après le dîner.
5. as fait une promenade.
6. sont restés chez eux.
7. ai réussi à l'examen.

F. **Conseils.**
1. c   3. c
2. a   4. a

G. **Message.**
Chers amis,
... Je n'ai pas envie de sortir. J'ai sommeil
tout le temps; je dors 12 heures par jour!
En plus, je ne mange pas, je n'ai pas faim.
Pourtant, je bois 3 litres d'eau par jour, j'ai
soif tout le temps! Le médecin dit que je dois
rester au lit pendant un mois —j'espère qu'il
a tort! J'ai besoin (j'ai envie) de voir...
Je vous embrasse. (XOXO)

H. **Le week-end dernier.** (*Sample answers; answers
will vary.*)
Le week-end dernier, je suis sorti(e) avec des
amis. Nous sommes allé(e)s au restaurant.
J'ai rencontré un garçon (une fille)
charmant(e). J'ai oublié mon livre de français
au restaurant. Je n'ai pas étudié pour l'exam-
en de français.

Unit Test 5B

A. **Dates historiques.**
1. 1066   3. 1789   5. 2002
2. 1431   4. 1945

B. **Voyage au présent ou voyage au passé?**
1. PC   3. PC   5. PC
2. P   4. PC   6. P

C. **Combien?**
1. S   3. P   5. P
2. S   4. S

D. **Une question de culture.**
1. V   3. F   5. V
2. V   4. F

E. **Hier aussi.**
1. a eu sommeil.
2. ont bien dormi.
3. n'a pas neigé.
4. avez fait la connaissance de quelqu'un.
5. sont allés au cinéma.
6. ai attendu le bus.
7. avons perdu notre temps.

F. **Conseils.**
1. a   3. a
2. b   4. c

G. **Message.**
Cher Jean-Pierre (Chère Marie-France),
Je sais que je suis très jeune; j'ai 18 ans
et tu as 22 ans, mais j'ai besoin de te parler
de mes sentiments. Tu es un garçon (une
fille) formidable et je crois que tu me
trouves bien aussi. Est-ce que j'ai raison
(j'ai tort)? Maintenant, tu rentres en France
et j'ai peur que tu trouves un(e) autre
petit(e) ami(e)! Est-ce que tu as l'intention
de m'envoyer du courrier électronique de
France? J'espère que oui. J'ai envie de rester
en contact avec toi.
Ton ami(e) que t'aime,

H. **Le week-end dernier.** (*Sample answers; answers
will vary.*)
Le weekend dernier, je suis allé(e) au cinéma.
J'ai rendu visite à une copine. J'ai beaucoup
dormi. J'ai étudié un peu. Dimanche, je suis
resté(e) à la maison.

Aperçu culturel: La France et ses régions (Version 5A)

A. **Quatre régions françaises.**
1. la Normandie
2. Paris
3. la Provence
4. l'Alsace

B. **L'histoire et les régions.**
1. b   4. c   7. a
2. a   5. c   8. b
3. c   6. a

C. **Un voyage imaginaire.** (*Answers will vary.*)

Aperçu culturel: La France et ses régions (Version 5B)

A. Quatre régions françaises.
1. l'Alsace
2. Paris
3. la Normandie
4. la Provence

B. L'histoire et les régions.

1. c	4. a	7. b
2. a	5. b	8. a
3. b	6. b	

C. Un voyage imaginaire. (*Answers will vary.*)

Unit Test 6A

A. Combien?

1. P	3. S	5. S
2. P	4. P	

B. Présent ou passé?

1. PC	3. PC	5. P
2. PC	4. P	

C. Vrai ou faux?

1. F	3. V	5. V
2. F	4. F	6. V

D. Questions personnelles. (*Sample answers; answers will vary.*)
1. Je bois du café et du jus d'orange au petit déjeuner.
2. J'ai moins d'argent que mes copains.
3. J'ai trop de travail pour la classe de français.
4. Oui, j'ai déjà voyagé en Europe.

E. Un repas d'anniversaire. (*Sample answers; answers may vary.*)
1. du jambon.
2. de la sole.
3. des haricots verts.
4. de la glace au chocolat.
5. de l'eau minérale et du vin.

F. Le champagne.

1. de	4. de	7. Le
2. le	5. le	8. du
3. de	6. du	

G. Où ça?

1. b	3. b	5. c
2. a	4. a	6. c

H. Composition: Joséphine est en excellente forme. (*Sample answers; answers will vary.*)

Two things she does:
1. Elle boit beaucoup d'eau.
2. Elle fait du sport et elle va à la gym.

Two things she doesn't do:
1. Elle ne mange pas beaucoup de pain.
2. Elle ne boit pas de bière.

Unit Test 6B

A. Combien?

1. S	3. P	5. S
2. P	4. P	

B. Présent ou passé?

1. P	3. PC	5. P
2. P	4. PC	

C. Vrai ou faux?

1. F	3. F	5. F
2. V	4. F	6. V

D. Questions personnelles. (*Sample answers; answers will vary.*)
1. Non, je ne bois pas de lait avec le dîner.
2. Je mange moins de légumes que mes parents.
3. Oui, je mange des fruits tous les jours.
4. Oui, j'ai déjà voyagé au Mexique.

E. Un repas romantique. (*Sample answers; answers will vary.*)
1. du saucisson (du caviar).
2. du saumon.
3. des petits pois.
4. du gâteau.
5. du champagne et du vin.

F. Le Coca.

1. le	4. du	7. du
2. de	5. de	8. de
3. du	6. le, le	

G. Où ça?

1. c	3. a	5. c
2. a	4. b	6. a

H. Composition: Yannick est trop maigre (*skinny*)!
1. Il mange beaucoup de viande.
2. Il fait beaucoup de jogging.

3. Il va souvent à la gym.
4. Il mange beaucoup de glace.

Unit Test 7A

A. Logique ou illogique?

1. L	3. I	5. L
2. I	4. I	

B. Les étudiants universitaires.

1. S	4. S	7. S
2. S	5. P	8. P
3. S/P	6. P	

C. L'éducation en France.

1. F	3. V	5. V
2. V	4. F	6. F

D. Questions: la vie à l'université. (*Sample answers; anwers may vary.*)
1. Oui, je le connais.
2. Non, je ne le trouve pas difficile.
3. Oui, je les comprends.
4. Oui, je la regarde souvent.
5. Non, je ne leur écris pas souvent.
6. Oui, ils me téléphonent souvent.

E. Mais non!
1. ne le cherche pas.
2. ne les écoute pas.
3. ne vais pas lui écrire.
4. ne leur ai pas parlé.
5. ne l'invitons pas ce soir.

F. Vous êtes fascinant(e)! (*Sample answers; answers may vary.*)
1. Je prépare un diplôme d'anglais.
2. Je suis cinq cours.
3. Ma bande dessinée préférée est *Astérix*.
4. Oui, j'ai lu un roman récemment. J'ai lu *Pluie et vent sur Télumée Miracle*.

G. Des conseils.

1. b	3. a	5. a
2. c	4. d	

H. Isidore Intello. (*Sample answers; answers will vary.*)
Isidore Intello suit des cours de philosophie et de littérature italienne. Ses cours sont très difficiles. Il lit Nietzche quand il a du temps libre. Le week-end il étudie à la bibliothèque. Les autres étudiants le trouvent un peu pénible, mais ils adorent son accent.

Unit Test 7B

A. Logique ou illogique?

1. L	3. L	5. I
2. I	4. L	

B. Les étudiants universitaires.

1. P	4. S/P	7. S/P
2. P	5. P	8. S
3. S	6. S	

C. L'éducation en France.

1. V	3. F	5. V
2. V	4. F	6. F

D. Questions: la vie à l'université. (*Sample answers; answers will vary.*)
1. Oui, je l'aime beaucoup.
2. Oui, ils m'aiment bien.
3. Non, je ne l'apprends pas.
4. Oui, je lui pose des questions.
5. Oui, je leur téléphone souvent.
6. Non, il ne m'en écrit pas.

E. Mais non!
1. ne les aide pas.
2. ne la dis pas.
3. ne vais pas la raconter.
4. ne lui ai pas envoyé de carte.
5. ne leur téléphonons pas.

F. Vous êtes fascinant(e)! (*Sample answers; answers will vary.*)
1. Après l'université je peux enseigner ou travailler dans un laboratoire.
2. Je veux enseigner.
3. Je suis des cours de biologie, de philosophie, d'histoire et de français.
4. Oui, j'ai envoyé un e-mail. J'ai envoyé un e-mail à ma mère.

G. Des conseils.

1. c	3. b	5. c
2. a	4. c	

H. Hippolyte Lamoureux. (*Sample answers; answers will vary.*)
Il suit un cours de maths très facile et un cours de tennis. Il lit *People* magazine quand il a du temps libre. Le week-end, il regarde la télévision, il dort et il fait la fête. Les autres étudiants le trouvent très amusant.

Aperçu culturel: Culture et loisirs (Version 7A)

A. Vrai ou faux?
1. V   4. V   6. V
2. V   5. V   7. F
3. F

B. Qu'en savez-vous?
1. c   4. b   6. b
2. a   5. a   7. a
3. a

C. Allons en France! (*Answers will vary.*)

Aperçu culturel: Culture et loisirs (Version 7B)

A. Vrai ou faux?
1. F   4. F   6. F
2. V   5. V   7. V
3. F

B. Qu'en savez-vous?
1. b   4. b   6. c
2. a   5. a   7. a
3. a

C. À vous de jouer! (*Answers will vary.*)

Unit Test 8A

A. Passé composé ou imparfait?
1. I   3. PC   5. PC
2. I   4. PC

B. La vie en France.
1. V   3. V   5. F
2. F   4. F   6. V

C. Autrefois. (*Sample answers; answers will vary.*)
1. Oui, j'habitais en banlieue quand j'étais petit(e).
2. Non, je ne parlais pas d'autres langues.
3. Mon dessin animé favori était *Scooby Doo.*
4. Oui, je lisais beaucoup.

D. Qui? Quoi? Comment?
1. Sais-tu   3. Connais-tu
2. Sais-tu   4. Connais-tu

E. Un événement étrange.
1. que   3. qu'
2. qui   4. que

F. Vous êtes unique au monde! (*Sample answers; answers will vary.*)
1. Dans les grandes villes il y a des musées, des cinémas et de bons restaurants.
2. Quand j'avais cinq ans, je vivais dans le Michigan.
3. Non, je ne sais pas chanter.
4. Ce matin à 8h je dormais.

G. Le rendez-vous.
1. aimait   5. a fait
2. était   6. ont compris
3. ont décidé 7. était
4. a regardé   8. sont rentrés

H. Le dîner romantique de Roméo et Juliette.
(*Sample answers; answers will vary.*)
Une fois, Roméo a décidé d'inviter Juliette dans un grand restaurant français pour son repas d'anniversaire. D'habitude, ils mangeaient chez MacDo. Ils ont parlé pendant longtemps de leur futur. Puis ils ont bien mangé. Finalement, le serveur a apporté l'addition. Soudain Roméo a remarqué qu'il avait laissé son portefeuille à la maison.

Unit Test 8B

A. Passé composé ou imparfait?
1. PC   3. I   5. PC
2. I   4. I

B. La vie en France.
1. F   3. V   5. V
2. V   4. F   6. V

C. Autrefois. (*Sample answers; answers will vary.*)
1. Oui, je regardais souvent la télévision.
2. Mon feuilleton favori était *Beverly Hills 90210.*
3. J'habitais en Californie quand j'avais cinq ans.
4. Non, nous ne partions pas souvent en vacances.

D. Qui? Quoi? Comment?
1. Connais-tu   3. Connais-tu
2. Sais-tu   4. Sais-tu

E. Un accident.
1. qui
2. qu'
3. qui
4. que

F. Vous êtes unique au monde! (*Sample answers; answers will vary.*)
1. Je préfère vivre en ville.
2. Je vis en banlieue.
3. Oui, je sais danser.
4. Non, je n'avais jamais étudié le français avant d'arriver à l'université.

G. La soucoupe volante. (*The UFO*).
1. était
2. faisait
3. est sorti
4. a vu
5. est descendue
6. portait
7. a pris
8. est parti

H. La fête de Fredy Fêtard. (*Sample answers; answers will vary.*)
Samedi une fête a eu lieu chez Fredy Fêtard. D'abord, tout le monde dansait et mangeait. Tout à coup un autre groupe d'étudiants est arrivé chez Fredy. Il ne les connaissait pas. Puis un ami de Fredy est tombé malade. Fredy l'a amené à l'hôpital. Pendant que Fredy était à l'hôpital la police est arrivée chez lui. Finalement, Fredy est rentré à la maison.

Unit Test 9A

A. Singulier ou pluriel?
1. P
2. S/P
3. S/P
4. S
5. P
6. S ou P
7. P

B. La vie en France.
1. F
2. V
3. F
4. V
5. V
6. F

C. Activités.
1. Tu t'habilles.
2. Ils se brossent les cheveux.
3. Elle se promène.
4. Nous nous rasons.

D. Suggestions et conseils.
1. Habille-toi!
2. Ne vous énervez pas!
3. Excuse-toi!
4. Ne te trompe pas!

E. De la tête aux pieds!
1. a
2. b
3. b
4. c
5. b

F. Hier.
1. Ils se sont rencontrés.
2. J'ai découvert la vérité.
3. Jacqueline s'est amusée.
4. Émilie et Carole se sont perdues.
5. Nous nous sommes donné rendez-vous.
6. Vous vous êtes parlé.
7. Tu t'es mis(e) en colère.

G. Transformations.
1. Nous ne nous y intéressons pas.
2. Est-ce que vous en avez en France?
3. J'en ai pris un.
4. Marc et Henri vont y passer la soirée.
5. Achetons-en pour la fête!

H. Dimanche matin. (*Answers will vary.*)

Unit Test 9B

A. Singulier ou pluriel?
1. S
2. S/P
3. P
4. S
5. P
6. P
7. P

B. La vie en France.
1. F
2. V
3. F
4. V
5. F
6. V

C. Activités.
1. me brosse les dents.
2. nous lavons.
3. te rases.
4. vous peignez.

D. Suggestions et conseils.
1. Repose-toi!
2. Dépêchez-vous!
3. Assieds-toi!
4. Ne vous levez pas!

E. De la tête aux pieds!
1. c
2. a
3. b
4. c
5. a

F. Hier.
1. Marc a ouvert la fenêtre.
2. Sylvie a couru cinq kilomètres.
3. Tu t'es couché(e) à minuit.

4. Nous nous sommes réveillé(e)s à sept heures.
5. Fatima s'est promenée en ville.
6. Pierre s'est lavé les cheveux.
7. Je me suis trompé(e).

G. Transformations.
1. Nicole n'en a pas peur.
2. Est-ce que tu y vas ce soir?
3. Marc en a acheté un kilo.
4. Tu n'y as pas écrit ton nom.
5. N'y retournons jamais!

H. Samedi soir. (*Answers will vary.*)

Aperçu culturel: La France, mère des arts (Version 9A)

A. Vrai ou faux?

1. V	4. F	6. V
2. F	5. F	7. F
3. V		

B. Qu'en savez-vous?

1. a	4. a	6. a
2. c	5. c	7. a
3. a		

C. La France, mère des arts. (*Answers will vary.*)

Aperçu culturel: La France, mère des arts (Version 9B)

A. Vrai ou faux?

1. V	4. V	6. V
2. F	5. V	7. V
3. F		

B. Qu'en savez-vous?

1. a	4. c	6. b
2. c	5. a	7. a
3. b		

C. L'art et l'artiste. (*Answers will vary.*)

Unit Test 10A

A. La rencontre.

ponctuellement	brillamment
patiemment	sérieusement
évidemment	poliment
gentiment	

(*Sample answers; answers may vary.*)
1. Oui, il arrive à l'heure. Il arrive à 4h et on dit qu'il est ponctuel.
2. Véronique et Chantal arrivent en retard parce qu'elles ont raté leur bus.
3. Non, Pierre n'est pas fâché quand les filles arrivent. Il répond gentiment que ça va quand Véronique s'excuse.
4. Oui, elle en sait quelque chose. Elle parle brillamment du cinéma.
5. Oui, Chantal en sait quelque chose aussi. Elle sait discuter sérieusement la cinématographie.
6. Non, Pierre ne parle pas trop; il écoute Chantal poliment.
7. Oui, il commence à s'intéresser à Chantal. C'est parce qu'elle est intelligente.

B. La vie en France.

1. V	3. V	5. V
2. F	4. F	6. F

C. L'immeuble de Chantal.

1. deuxième	4. huitième
2. quatrième	5. cinquième
3. premier	6. troisième

D. La carte postale.
Bonjour Martine!
... en juin, tu <u>verras</u> qu'il est très beau! Nous <u>ferons</u> des matches de tennis ensemble. Est-ce que tu aimes le jazz? Nous <u>aurons</u> l'occasion d'assister au Festival de musique à Aix-en-Provence si ça t'intéresse. Le Festival <u>durera</u> tout le mois de juin. J'ai une voiture donc (*therefore*), je <u>pourrai</u> conduire si tu veux.
Amitiés,
Chantal

E. Au téléphone.

1. c	3. c	5. b
2. b	4. b	

F. Composition guidée. (*Answers will vary.*)

Unit Test 10B

A. La cérémonie.

malheureusement	attentivement
constamment	seulement
calmement	finalement
sérieusement	longuement
vraiment	

1. Oui, il est ponctuel. Il est arrivé en avance comme d'habitude.

2. Il regarde constamment sa montre.
3. Elle lui a dit qu'elle voulait passer le reste de sa vie avec lui.
4. Il pense qu'elle a changé d'avis parce qu'elle parle souvent de son voisin.
5. Il croit qu'elle s'intéresse à Bob parce qu'elle l'écoute toujours très attentivement.
6. Quand elle arrive, elle regarde Marc longuement avec amoir.
7. Oui, ils se marient. Leur nouvelle vie de couple commence.

B. La vie en France.
1. V   3. F   5. F
2. V   4. V   6. V

C. Les faire-part.
1. onzième   4. seizième
2. premier   5. huitième
3. troisième   6. dix-neuvième

D. La lune de miel.
Chère Carole,
      Nous avons décidé; nous <u>irons</u> en Guadeloupe en lune de miel. Nous <u>partirons</u> de Paris le 25 juin. Là-bas nous <u>ferons</u> des promenades romantiques sur les belles plages. Pendant notre séjour, il y <u>aura</u> un festival de musique zouk. On <u>pourra</u> aussi connaître la cuisine des îles. Je t'<u>enverrai</u> une carte postale!...
Amitiés,
Élodie

E. Au téléphone.
1. c   3. b   5. b
2. a   4. a

F. Composition guidée. (*Answers will vary.*)

Unit Test 11A

A. Avant de partir.
fasse, prenne, soient, aille, soyons, ait, vienne, puissions, ayons

1. F   3. V   5. V
2. F   4. F

B. Les Québécois, les Européens et la technologie.
1. V   4. V   6. V
2. F   5. F   7. V
3. V

C. Au contraire! (*Answers will vary.*)
1. ... les Européens soient indépendants.

2. ... les universités américaines aient beaucoup d'argent.
3. ... il y ait trop de violence au cinéma.
4. ... les Américains travaillent trop.

D. Questions personnelles. (*Sample answers; answers may vary.*)
1. J'en parle trois <u>ou</u> je parle trois langues.
2. Oui, il est possible que je vote dans les prochaines élections présidentielles.
3. Oui, il est indispensable qu'on respecte les minorités.
4. Oui, j'y crois <u>ou</u> je crois à l'horoscope.
5. Oui, je crois que mes parents sont intelligents.

E. Des conseils. (*Sample answers; answers may vary.*)
1. Il faut que tu étudies beaucoup.
2. Il est essentiel que tu suives des cours intéressants.
3. Il vaut mieux que tu sois sérieux.
4. Je souhaite que tu te fasses des amis.
5. Je sais que tu vas aller à beaucoup de fêtes.
6. J'ai peur que tu dormes toute la journée.

F. Le Canada et les États-Unis.
1. c   3. b
2. a   4. a

G. Tous les pronoms du monde. (*Sample answers; correct answers may be affirmative or negative.*)
1. Non, je ne les leur prête pas.
2. Oui, je m'en sers.
3. Oui, je lui en envoie souvent.
4. Oui, il y en a.
5. Non, je ne m'y intéresse pas.

H. Aimez-vous les cadeaux?
1. Oui, donnez-la-moi!
2. Non, ne me l'offrez pas!
3. Oui, prétez-m'en!

Unit Test 11B

A. Vive la France profonde!
perde, quittions, retrouve, puisse, veuille, aient, fasse, soit, comprenne

1. V   3. V   5. F
2. V   4. V

B. Les Québécois, les Européens et la technologie.
1. F   4. F   6. F
2. V   5. V   7. V
3. V

C. Au contraire!
1. ... tous les Américains soient riches.
2. ... Haïti ait une économie stable.
3. ... toute la musique rap soit violente.
4. ... il y ait des Européens très traditionnels.

D. Questions personnelles. (*Sample answers; answers may vary.*)
1. J'en suis cinq.
2. Oui, il est important que j'apprenne une autre langue.
3. Oui, il est normal que les États-Unis aident les pays pauvres.
4. Non, il n'est pas nécessaire que je sois riche un jour.
5. Non, je ne crois pas que mes parents aient toujours raison.

E. Des conseils. (*Sample answers; answers may vary.*)
1. Il est préférable que tu te fasses des amis francophones.
2. Il est important que tu sois à l'heure au travail.
3. Il est indispensable que tu puisses utiliser ton français.

4. Je suis fier(fière) que tu partes au Québec cet été.
5. Je suis content(e) que tu veuilles aller à Montréal.
6. Je veux que tu ailles voir des films français.

F. Vive le progrès!

1. a	3. c
2. b	4. a

G. Tous les pronoms du monde. (*Sample answers; correct answers may be affirmative or negative.*)
1. Non, je ne vous en prête pas.
2. Non, je ne leur en écris pas souvent.
3. Non, je n'aimerais pas l'être.
4. Oui, il y en a au cinéma de ma ville.
5. Oui, j'en ai beaucoup.

H. Vous vous y intéressez? (*Sample answers; correct answers may be affirmative or negative.*)
1. Oui. Donne-le-lui!
2. Oui. Présente-les-moi!
3. Non. Ne la lui donne pas!

VIVRE EN FRANCE ORAL TESTS

General Guidelines

The Tests: The **Vivre en France** tests are a series of oral exams that focus on the practical vocabulary and survival skills found in the **Vivre en France** sections of the seventh edition of *Contacts*. They provide students with the opportunity to interact with each other in authentic situations, using the target language to carry out specific tasks. Each exam can be completed within one class period and can save instructors class time, while allowing them to evaluate their students' oral skills on a regular basis.

Observing/Recording: As students are working in groups simultaneously, the instructor will not be able to observe each and every interaction. They will instead collect samples of the various interactions from different groups. This can be done by circulating from group to group, taking notes on performance, or by videotaping students. With a large class, it is preferable to enlist the help of a colleague, so that you are both either filming or taking notes on different groups at the same time. Unless otherwise noted, the instructor films or observes a sample of all sections of each exam for each student.

Grading: The "grade sheet" is to be completed by the instructor. It may be helpful to film students or take notes on them during the exam, and then to use the video and/or notes to analyze and grade the results at a later time. As the exact focus or number of interactions to be graded varies from test to test due to the nature and complexity of the role plays, it is important to note these differences beforehand. For all exams, one point is to be deducted each time a student resorts to English during the exam.

Format: There are four possible formats: 1) one-on-one student/teacher interaction (the least common); 2) pair work; 3) small group work (usually groups of three); 4) mingling spontaneous interaction between many different groupings, within a set period of time (much like a party). When interacting one-on-one, students enter the classroom individually and respond to the instructor's questions. In pair work, pairs may be assigned ahead (unless the activity requires working in as many different pairs as possible). In groups of three, students are designated Student A, Student B, and Student C. Student A initiates a conversation with Student B. Student B responds. Student B initiates the next interchange with Student C, and so on.

Preparation: The exercises in **Vivre en France** provide excellent practice beforehand. If time allows, it is ideal to designate the class before as "practice and preparation" for the exam. Student pairs can be assigned at that time, and students will have the opportunity to familiarize themselves with the exam's format. As a result, the class test will run much more smoothly.

Choosing Small Group and Pair Work Partners: It is preferable to pair (or group) students with classmates with whom they do not ordinarily work. In groups of three, two strong, or relatively strong, and one weak student per group is best. In pairs, do not group the weakest student of the class with the strongest; both will be frustrated. Students are best paired with those closer to their own strength. On occasion, pairing two very strong students together can allow them both to do their best work and to challenge themselves. It is important to give some thought to the groupings prior to the actual test.

Student Reaction: Students may, at first, balk at the idea of an oral exam, and of being videotaped. A practice session during the preceding class can help to demystify the process for them. During the exam itself, as students interact with each other, they tend to forget the presence of the camera or the instructor. This may be one of the most enjoyable experiences students have in your class!

Unit 1

A. Classroom etiquette (in groups of three). You are not sure your classmates have understood what classroom etiquette is all about in French. Choose five of the following to test their knowledge. Continue your discussion until everyone has answered five different questions.

1. You have the best accent in your class and the teacher needs someone to read a poem by Jacques Prévert. What does your teacher say to you?

2. Your teacher asks you what color scarf Madame Bovary was wearing when she left her husband. What do you respond?

3. You know your teacher loves you to be polite. What do you say when you ask for an "A" in the course?

4. Your new French penpal (whom you met over the Internet) says that you are "vachement chouette." You would like to know what that means before you respond. What do you ask him/her?

5. You are determined to never utter another word of English in French class. You do, however, need to know how you say "bathroom" in French. What do you ask?

6. Your teacher has been speaking nonstop for ten minutes. You think she is speaking Wolof, an African dialect. What do you say to show that you are lost?

7. Your teacher has brought in his/her slides from his/her last trip to France. What does he/she ask the class to do?

8. You have to borrow a pen from your partner. What word do you have to use to ask politely?

9. Your teacher is going to give you a dictation. What does he/she ask you to do in order to have something to write on?

10. Your teacher asks you a question and he/she wants an answer. What does he/she say to you?

11. Your best friend is about to be called on in class and you can tell he/she is daydreaming. What do you say?

12. Your teacher puts a cassette in the tape recorder. What does he/she ask the class to do as he/she plays it?

13. Your teacher wants all the students to follow along in the book as he/she reads. What does he/she say?

14. Your partner has just answered another difficult question correctly. What does the teacher say to him/her?

15. You asked your partner his/her name and instead he/she told you where he/she lives. What do you say to him/her?

Vivre en France Oral Tests, Unit 1 **VF 3**

NOM _____ CLASSE _____ DATE _____

Unit 1   GRADE SHEET

A. Classroom etiquette.

Grade students in each category for each question.

1.	Appropriate responses	10	9	8	7	6
	Pronunciation	5	4	3	2	1
	Naturalness, fluency	5	4	3	2	1
2.	Appropriate responses	10	9	8	7	6
	Pronunciation	5	4	3	2	1
	Naturalness, fluency	5	4	3	2	1
3.	Appropriate responses	10	9	8	7	6
	Pronunciation	5	4	3	2	1
	Naturalness, fluency	5	4	3	2	1
4.	Appropriate responses	10	9	8	7	6
	Pronunciation	5	4	3	2	1
	Naturalness, fluency	5	4	3	2	1
5.	Appropriate responses	10	9	8	7	6
	Pronunciation	5	4	3	2	1
	Naturalness, fluency	5	4	3	2	1

Maintaining a conversation in French. (10 points)

One point will be deducted each time English is used in the course of the test. _____

TOTAL GRADE = _____/100

Vivre en France Oral Tests, Unit 1   **VF   5**

Unit 2

A. Introductions (one on one). Your instructor wants to get to know you better. Reintroduce yourself to him/her and answer his/her questions about you. Then introduce the next classmate in line to your instructor.

B. Inviting friends (mingling). Speak to as many other students as possible to fill up your social calendar (below). You will be inviting others and accepting and declining invitations. When someone accepts your invitation, write his/her name in the appropriate box below, along with the activity and when you will meet (10h, 14h, etc.).

Pour chaque rendez-vous, indiquez:

- • le jour   • l'heure   • la personne   • l'activité

MON CALENDRIER		
vendredi	**samedi**	**dimanche**

Vivre en France Oral Tests, Unit 2   **VF** 7